MEETING NEEDS
SHARING CHRIST

Ministry Evangelism in Today's New Testament Church

DONALD A. ATKINSON &
CHARLES L. ROESEL

LifeWay Press
Nashville, Tennessee

7200-39
ISBN 0-8054-9842-7

Dewey Decimal Classification: 269.2
Subject Headings: EVANGELISTIC WORK // WITNESSING //
CHRISTIAN SOCIAL MINISTRY

Unless indicated otherwise, Scripture quotations are from
the Holy Bible, *New International Version*,
copyright © 1973, 1978, 1984
by International Bible Society.

Scripture quotations marked GNB are from the *Good News Bible,*
The Bible in Today's English Version.
Old Testament: Copyright © American Bible Society 1976;
New Testament: Copyright © American Bible Society 1966, 1971, 1976.
Used by permission.

Printed in the United States of America

LifeWay Press
127 Ninth Avenue, North
Nashville, Tennessee 37234

For seven years Joan McCullen served with her husband, Dave, as director of the Rescue Mission at First Baptist Church, Leesburg, Florida. Joan's ministry came to a tragic end on March 25, 1995, in a head-on collision with a car driven by a young man under the influence of alcohol. To the more than 1,500 men who passed through the mission during Joan's ministry, she was a mother and a friend who lovingly opened her heart and her home to anyone in need. Joan's life exemplified the concept of ministry evangelism and stands as a model for all who would take up their crosses and follow Christ in her footsteps. This book is dedicated to her memory.

The Authors

Charles Roesel (left) and
Donald Atkinson

DONALD A. ATKINSON came to work at the Sunday School Board of the Southern Baptist Convention in Nashville, Tennessee, in 1983 after serving as the pastor of Baptist churches in Alabama, Georgia, and Kentucky. His work at the Sunday School Board has included both editorial and consulting responsibilities. A native of Huntsville, Alabama, he attended Samford University and is a graduate of Athens College (B.A.), the Southern Baptist Theological Seminary (B.D., M.Div.), and New Orleans Baptist Theological Seminary (D.Min.). Atkinson is the author of *A Barnabas Lifestyle* and *Celebrating Life*. He has also written numerous articles and study resources. In addition to his duties at the Sunday School Board, Don serves as the pastor of Walker Memorial Baptist Church in Franklin, Tennessee.

CHARLES L. ROESEL has been the pastor of First Baptist Church, Leesburg, Florida, since 1976. Under his leadership the church has become a leading evangelistic church in the Southern Baptist Convention, baptizing more than three hundred persons each year. Roesel is a graduate of Stetson University (B.A.) and the Southern Baptist Theological Seminary (B.D.). Active in denominational life, he has served as the president of the Florida Baptist Pastors Conference and as a member of the Executive Committee of the Southern Baptist Convention. Roesel is a nationally known preacher and conference leader in the areas of evangelism and church growth.

Contents

Preface

MEMBERS OF THE ADULT 4 DEPARTMENT knew how to have a party, but this time they had outdone themselves. The church's fellowship hall was festive, with red, gold, and green Christmas decorations. So much food had been prepared that three long banquet tables were required to display all of it, including turkey, ham, dressing, a variety of vegetables, and many salads. Best of all, an entire table was required for the desserts.

Pastors are blessed! They are almost always invited to big church parties. I had just given thanks for the food when the party was momentarily interrupted by a poorly dressed street person who had wandered into the banquet hall. One member quickly met him near the door. As the raggedly dressed man waited, the member who had talked with him came to the table where the others stood waiting to serve themselves. The man was hungry. Could we prepare a plate for him? The organizer of the meal answered: "Yes, we probably can; but let everyone else go through the line first. Then, if we have enough left, we will prepare a plate for him."

An awkward silence followed until someone finally spoke up: "No, we will prepare for this man first. Then the rest of us will eat." Hastily, a plate was filled with food, and hot coffee was poured. A place was prepared for the man, and several persons made certain his needs were met. One member made sure he would have a place to sleep that night. Only then did we resume our party. But nothing could undo what we had done. We had gathered to have our feast. When a needy person intruded on our celebration, we thought of ourselves first. To make matters worse, we had acted this way toward a needy person at a celebration of the Savior's birth!

Sad but true, this story of our failure and of our lack of sensitivity is a kind of parable of the church in today's world. Too often, persons who are hurting and who are on the edges of society interrupt the work of today's church. We have buildings to build, budgets to raise, and numerical goals to reach. Persons who do not fit the profile of our congregation are considered an interruption. Some of them do not dress, act, or smell like our kind. Many have serious problems that scare us even to think about. Besides, we do not have the resources to deal with all of these persons—not if we are going to carry on our programs. We serve ourselves first. If anything is left after we fulfill our needs, we might help others—but even then from a distance. We might support the clothes closet, the food bank, or the rescue mission. But we don't really touch individuals; instead, we minister to persons at arm's length.

Jesus' attitude was different from that of many church members today. He spent time with persons and poured out His life for those who were sinful and broken. He was concerned about physical as well as spiritual needs. He often spoke a word of forgiveness to persons who were in the bondage of sin, but He also cared about their physical and emotional well-being. For example, when Jesus looked at a huge crowd of people who had come to hear Him teach, He was concerned about their need for food. With a boy's lunch of five barley loaves and two small fish, Jesus fed the crowd (see John 6:5-13). Because the people's hunger was important to Jesus, He used His power to meet their need.

This book is about ministering to persons up close and face-to-face. More and more churches are coming to understand what it means to be the body of Christ in a broken world. To such churches, business as usual is not good enough. A hunger is emerging in many Christians to go beyond the protective walls of the sanctuary into a world that is sometimes dirty and dangerous. Many Christians want to make a difference for the masses of hurting people who walk our streets, travel our highways, share our neighborhoods, and sometimes sit in our pews. This study is intended as a resource for these believers and their churches.

We call the concept presented in this study ministry evangelism. This designation is important because social ministry alone is not the church's purpose. Helping persons in need is admirable. A debt of gratitude is due all of the churches, social-service agencies, and individuals who try to help persons; but the church has a greater responsibility than feeding, clothing, or housing needy persons. More than anything, persons need the saving gospel of Jesus. Ministry evangelism is meeting persons' needs in order to share God's love and forgiveness with them. Although ministry is always given unconditionally, it is never given without sharing the reason for it all—God's love as demonstrated through the Lord Jesus Christ.

First Baptist Church, Leesburg, Florida, is one congregation that practices ministry evangelism. In fact, the term *ministry evangelism* originated at this church. Under the leadership of its pastor, Charles Roesel, this church has begun more than 70 different ministries. First Baptist's ministries are varied, but all of them are built on solid biblical and theological foundations. These ministries are designed to touch persons at the point of their need with the goal of introducing them to Jesus Christ as Savior and Lord.

This book has two authors, Donald Atkinson and Charles Roesel. We have spent time together. We have prayed together. We have shared the dream of introducing the principles of ministry evangelism to pastors, leaders, and all Christians who want to make a difference in persons' lives. Because we live about six hundred miles apart, working jointly has sometimes been difficult. The method employed was for Charles Roesel to provide as much information as possible about the concept and implementation of ministry evangelism and for Donald Atkinson to do the actual writing. Therefore, when the first person is used, it describes the personal experiences of Donald Atkinson. The words and experiences of Charles Roesel are identified and attributed to him. The reader will find both of us in this work because we have both put our hearts into it. We send it out with the fervent hope and prayer that God will use it to challenge His people to loving ministry evangelism.

1

Caring with a Difference

BOBBY SMITH'S ARTWORK was recently shown at the Leesburg, Florida, Arts Festival. Although this achievement sounds rather commonplace, it would not have been possible a few years ago. Bobby was an alcoholic who had spent several years on the streets of Orlando. When he heard about a rescue mission in Leesburg, an hour's drive away, he decided to investigate it. Sixteen months later he was working daily at the men's shelter. Speaking of his experience at the mission, one of more than 70 ministries of First Baptist Church, Leesburg, Smith says: "It's given me a new start. What I got here was love and direction, understanding, and patience."[1]

Leesburg, Florida, is much like thousands of other towns across the nation. Located about an hour from the excitement of Orlando, this central-Florida town of 25,000 has the feel and look of small-town USA, with tree-lined streets, a high-school football stadium, friendly people, well-kept homes, numerous churches, small businesses, and various fast-food restaurants. Leesburg is not a fast-growing town, having experienced a growth rate of only 6 percent over the past 10 years. It is a good place to live and rear a family but not the kind of setting in which you would expect to encounter a miracle.

First Baptist Church in Leesburg, until recent years, was as typical as the town. With attractive, well-kept buildings; a membership made up of a cross section of the population; and the usual church activities, First Baptist served Leesburg well. Many community and business leaders were members. The church's staff ministers were an important part of the community. Emphasizing Bible study, worship, youth activities, music, missions, and evangelism, the church resembled Southern Baptist churches in many small towns. Like most churches, First Baptist was experiencing limited growth. The church averaged about 300 persons in Sunday School attendance and added about 30 members a year through baptism. Most new members were relatives of families in the church; many were children who had grown up in the church. Like the town, First Baptist was hardly the setting in which you would expect a miracle. But that was 15 years ago.

The town of Leesburg has changed little in the past 15 years, but a revolution has taken place at First Baptist Church. The church sits on a grassy knoll with steps ascending to the columned portico. Through the brass-handled double doors passes each week a patchwork congregation that has been woven together by the threads of ministry evangelism. Unlike the traditional facade of its building, the church is anything but traditional or ordinary. Instead, it is a diverse fellowship, uniquely united in the bonds of Christ's love. There God is breaking down walls of separation and is building His kingdom in the hearts of His people.

The stately old doors that have served the church for so long are not wide enough these days. Now new doors of hope exist, through which pass the poor, the needy, the battered, the lonely, and the hurting. Ministries such as the Rescue Mission, the Women's Care Center, the Children's Shelter, the Pregnancy-Care Center, and the Benevolence Ministry serve the needs of troubled and needy persons who live on the fringes of society. Many professionals and affluent persons have found ministries such as the Christian school, day care, and after-school program to be their doors of entry to the church. The counseling and support-group ministries are doors of hope to the wounded and discouraged, within and outside the church membership. Hundreds of children crowd through the doors of Saturday Sunday School, Vacation Bible School, and the Latchkey Ministry. Senior adults find open doors in still other ministries. Hearing-impaired and deaf persons find a door of communication open to them. Even the imprisoned find an open door to caring ministry.

Ministry evangelism has brought many changes to the church. Church properties now include the original buildings plus 19 contiguous properties and buildings. The church's income has increased from $180,000 in 1979 to more than $2,000,000 annually. Most importantly, the church regularly baptizes more than 300 persons each year. A miracle has taken place in Leesburg, Florida. The members of First Baptist Church call the miracle ministry evangelism.

Ministry evangelism is not difficult to define, nor is it anything new. It is as old as the Christian faith. Ministry evangelism is simply caring for persons in the name of Jesus Christ. It is meeting persons at the point of their need and ministering to them physically and spiritually. The intent of ministry evangelism is to present the good news of God's love in order to introduce persons to Jesus. Ministry evangelism is not manipulative. Ministry is given lovingly and unconditionally. But the reason for it all, God's love for lost persons, is always shared. First Baptist, Leesburg, and many other churches have found that ministry evangelism is a biblical, Christ-centered, authentic, and loving way to bring persons to the Savior.

Ministry evangelism rests on strong biblical and theological foundations, specifically, the biblical doctrines of the incarnation and the priesthood of believers. The incarnation means that God has chosen to be vitally involved with human need. This involvement has always been part of God's nature and character, but it comes into clear focus in Jesus' coming in human flesh. The priesthood of believers is the biblical description of the way God wants His people to relate to others. God's call is always more than a call to blessing and privilege. It is a call to be a priest to others, to bring them to God. God's people in both the Old and New Testaments are called to be priests to others. History shows that God's people can too easily forget this calling, coming to see themselves as favored by God without seeing themselves as God's representatives.

Ministry evangelism grows from our understanding of God as an incarnational, relating God and our understanding of ourselves, God's people, as God's ministers who are called to bring others to the Father's love.

INCARNATIONAL EVANGELISM: THE DIVINE PLAN

How can the church get the attention of the world's broken and sinful people? Findley B. Edge maintains: "It will have to be done primarily through a ministry of revealing Christ through our lives and witness. ... It will have to be done primarily through an incarnational ministry."[2]

Ministry evangelism is incarnational evangelism. The most important theological statement in the Bible is found in John 1:14: "The Word became flesh and made his dwelling among us." This truth is the foundation for understanding God's redemptive purpose in history. Jesus' resurrection is often called the chief Christian doctrine. Obviously, no gospel would exist apart from the resurrection. His resurrection validates everything He said and did, including His death on the cross for sin. Yet even the resurrection is based on the incarnation. The atonement and the resurrection have power because they were accomplished by the Word (God) that became flesh (man). The truth of the incarnation—that God took on human flesh—sets the Christian gospel apart from all other religions. All religions profess the existence of a supreme Being, and all have holy men and prophets; but only the Christian faith proclaims that God actually took on human flesh.

We should not be surprised that God chose to reveal Himself in human flesh. God's revelation of Himself was always incarnational in intention. From the beginning God involved Himself in the world He made. He called His creation good; and until sin built a barrier, He related personally to the humans He created. The Old Testament reveals God as holy and all-powerful. Yet incredibly, Abraham, one of the major figures in the Old Testament, was called God's friend (see Jas. 2:23). Clearly, from the very beginning God desired to have fellowship with the people He had made, to enter their lives in a deeply personal relationship, and to reveal Himself as a relating God, One who wishes to be known to His people.

God revealed Himself to people in Old Testament times. For example, He sought the love and obedience of His people, He revealed His will through the patriarchs and the prophets, and He provided for His people when they were in danger or in need. But in Jesus' coming into the world, God revealed Himself in human flesh. In the words of Paul, "When the time had fully come, God sent his Son, born of a woman" (Gal. 4:4). Jesus' humanity was not counterfeit. He was genuinely human. God actually clothed Himself in human flesh and became one of us. Even His death on the cross, which removed the barriers between God and humanity as well as among humanity, was accomplished "in his flesh," abolishing "the law with its commandments and regulations" (Eph. 2:15). In His human flesh Jesus died and bought our redemption with His blood.

Christians often do not take the incarnation seriously enough. Sometimes we talk and act as though God did not come in human flesh, imprisoning Him behind stained-glass windows and sanctuary walls. The Jesus of the New Testament was truly a human. He was born to a peasant woman and grew up in a poor home. He knew hunger, He wept, He enjoyed the company of His friends, He was tempted, and He felt pain. These facts do not deny the truth that He is God, but we must never forget that the Word became flesh. Any belief system about Jesus that does not confess His real humanity is heretical (see 1 John 4:2-3).

Jesus, the Word made flesh, calls His people to obedient witnessing and ministry in an incarnational way:

• Jesus said, " 'Follow me and I will make you fishers of men' " (Mark 1:17). "Follow me" is Jesus' command. "I will make you fishers of men" is His promise. If Christians are not fishers of persons, they are not following Jesus. Being a fisher of persons is more than being just a winner of souls. These persons have real lives with real needs in a real world, as well as a spiritual nature that transcends this world. To win a man or a woman to Christ is to win a whole person—body, mind, and spirit.

• Jesus said, " 'Go and make disciples of all nations ... and surely I am with you always, to the very end of the age' " (Matt. 28:19-20). This promise means that as we go about the business of making disciples, Jesus is with us all the way. A disciple is a follower of Jesus, a pupil enrolled in His school to learn and grow, someone who seeks to live the way Jesus lived. Discipleship has everything to do with incarnation. A disciple incarnates and fleshes out a commitment to Jesus in the present world of human need.

• Jesus said, " 'You will be my witnesses' " (Acts 1:8). Christian witnessing is not voluntary; neither is it simply mandatory. It is inevitable. If Christ is in our hearts, He will be in our talk. Witnesses confess to something they have seen, experienced, or touched. Far more is involved here than persuading persons to agree to a few propositions. Witnessing possesses the character of incarnation as the witnesses share what has happened in their lives.

Because God is relational and incarnational, He chose to create humans in His image (see Gen. 1:26-27). Being made in God's image means, among other things, that we are like God in our need to relate to Him and to one another. Humans are spiritual beings, but we are more. Our spiritual nature is incarnate in a body of flesh and blood. We need to relate not only to the God who made us but also to fellow humans. When God made Adam, He was concerned about his need for companionship, so He gave Adam a woman to be his marital partner (see Gen. 2:20-22). It was clear from the beginning, then, that humans need other humans. God, who is relational and incarnational, made us the same way. This is the reason ministry evangelism makes such an important theological statement. It is built on the incarnational nature of God, who reaches out to touch us even in our sin, and it is built on God's intention that our ministry to others be incarnational—that we relate to others person to person, face-to-face, touching them in their brokenness.

The pattern on which ministry evangelism is built is incarnational. God made us to be relational and incarnational. The gospel is a message of Jesus' incarnation in human flesh. The only way it can be biblically shared is to focus on whole persons, with all of their hurts and needs, and to involve the church in ministering to those persons and in leading them to Christ. This is the essence of ministry evangelism.

Nothing is unusual about a church that majors on evangelism. Pastor Charles Roesel often says that First Baptist Church of Leesburg exists for evangelism as a fire exists for burning. Winning persons to faith in Jesus Christ is the priority of many, if not most, evangelical churches. However, evangelism that does not minister to the needs of the whole person falls short of the New Testament standard. Evangelism is incarnational when it recognizes that the Christ who came in human flesh is concerned about persons—body, mind, and spirit. Evangelism that sees persons only as souls to be saved is deficient, at best; in light of the incarnation, it may even be considered unbiblical.

GOD'S CALL IS ALWAYS TO WITNESS AND MINISTER

In addition to the incarnation, ministry evangelism is rooted in the rich biblical doctrine of the priesthood of believers. God has always called His people to a redemptive mission. When God called Abram, the fountainhead of the Jewish nation, His call included the promise that God would make of Abram and his descendants a great nation with God's special blessings. Because God provided for the Hebrews, gave them His promises, and made them His own, Abram's descendants often basked in God's favor. Too often, Israel drew inside itself and away from the people of the world, seeming to forget that God's call through Abram decreed,

> "All peoples on earth
>   will be blessed through you" (Gen. 12:3).

This responsibility to bless others was reiterated many times. Specifically, God promised that His people, Israel, would be His " ' "treasured possession" ' " (Ex. 19:5). While this verse speaks of the privileges Israel enjoyed as God's chosen people, in the next verse God said, " ' "You will be for me a kingdom of priests" ' " (Ex. 19:6). The work of priests involves bringing people into relationship with God. In other words, God expected Israel to bring people of all nations into relationship with Him.

Israel's lack of understanding of its redemptive mission fills the Old Testament. Isaiah eloquently stated Israel's purpose:

> "I will also make you a light for the Gentiles,
>   that you may bring my salvation to the ends of the earth"
>   (Isa. 49:6).

Later, Isaiah gave Israel God's view of its religious practice, specifically fasting. Religious activities are not an end in themselves. God asked,

> "Is not this the kind of fasting I have chosen:
> to loose the chains of injustice
>   and untie the cords of the yoke,
> to set the oppressed free
>   and break every yoke?" (Isa. 58:6).

The message to Israel was clear. The practice of religion that does not result in social justice and the redemption of others is unacceptable to God.

Findley B. Edge reminds us that Israel's call by God involved three important roles:

• Israel was chosen to be the recipient of God's revelation of Himself.
• Israel was called to reflect God's character.
• Israel was called to be God's instrument to reveal Himself to all the peoples of the earth. As God revealed Himself to Israel through the patriarchs and the prophets, a certain degree of piety developed in the life of Israel, setting it apart from its idolatrous neighbors. But generally speaking, Israel failed in its priestly role of bringing God's redemptive love to the nations of the world. Sadly, Israel "tended to take God as her own exclusive possession and failed to carry out the divine purpose. Ignoring the pleas of the prophets, Israel persisted in her failure."[3]

All too often, religion becomes corrupted by focusing on itself and moving behind protective walls that are designed to serve *us* and to keep *them* out. By the time of Jesus' earthly ministry, the Jewish religion had become so narrowly focused that it seemed almost designed to keep out "undesirables." A Gentile could break into the system only with great effort. By becoming a God-fearer and then a proselyte, a Gentile who was tired of the emptiness of idolatry could, religiously, become a Jew. Relatively few persons took the initiative to do this, and Jewish religious leaders certainly made no concerted effort to reach out to Gentiles with redemptive love. These leaders were far more inclined to put persons in derogatory categories than to tell them of God's love. They spoke of sinners, Samaritans, tax collectors, people of the land, and Gentile dogs. They erected tall barriers to keep out such persons. After all, the Jews must have reasoned, they were God's people. Others did not really matter very much. Part of their hatred of Jesus grew from the fact that He was unaffected by the barriers they had erected. Gentiles, Samaritans, tax gatherers, prostitutes, lepers, women—all experienced Jesus' redemptive love. He obviously did not share the Jewish leaders' religious exclusivism. Nor was His ministry calculated to preserve the religious status quo.

Jesus' ministry was like a breath of fresh air. He healed the sick, comforted the afflicted, fed the hungry, and loved the unlovable. His approach to ministry was both incarnational and relational. He was and is God in the flesh, and He ministered person to person with compassion. Later in our study we will look closely at Jesus' ministry. But in summary, everything He said and did, including dying on a Roman cross, emanated from His love for persons and His desire to bring them into relationship with the Father.

The early church saw itself as God's new people. Peter wrote: "You are a chosen people, a royal priesthood, a holy nation, a people belonging to God, that you may declare the praises of him who called you out of darkness into his wonderful light. Once you were not a people, but now you are the people of God; once you had not received mercy, but now you have received mercy" (1 Pet. 2:9-10). The believers' conviction that they were God's priests became the foundation on which the church's ministry would be built.

The early church shared Jesus' passion for persons. The Book of Acts is a thrilling chronicle of evangelistic endeavor. Even when they were facing persecution and were forced to scatter from Jerusalem, those brave believers used their difficult circumstances to spread the good news about Jesus (see Acts 6:7). Although the initial preaching of the gospel was directed to Jews, these believers soon understood the truth that God loves all persons. A classic example of the zeal they demonstrated in bringing persons to Christ is the story of Philip and the Ethiopian, recorded in Acts 8. The Holy Spirit led Philip to travel the desert road to Gaza. There he saw a man in a chariot and noticed that he was reading. On closer examination he discovered that the man, an official of the Ethiopian queen, was reading from a scroll of Isaiah. Perhaps this man had tired of pagan religion and had decided to go to Jerusalem to learn more about the Jewish religion. Obviously, his questions had not been answered, even though he had taken the initiative to find the truth about God. When Philip asked the man if he understood what he was reading, he asked for Philip's help. The encounter that followed led the man to understand that the Scripture he was reading gave witness to Jesus. We do not know all that was said or how long the conversation lasted, but we know how it ended. The Ethiopian found the goal of his search in Jesus. Before Philip left, he baptized him as a confession of his newfound faith.

Because this man was wealthy and powerful, he needed no ministry such as food or shelter. But he was lost and needed someone who would be sensitive to his need. Philip was that person. That day in the desert the Word became flesh as Philip shared Christ face-to-face with the Ethiopian. This story illustrates what these early believers did constantly. They made it their business to be out on the paths of life, always watching for opportunities to point someone to faith in Jesus. The Book of Acts depicts evangelism as engaged and involved with persons wherever they were. The approach of the earliest church, like that of its Lord, was incarnational. It was warm-blooded, personal, and effective.

No event in church history is more significant than the conversion of

Saul of Tarsus. Saul was brilliant, aggressive, and convinced of the validity of his opposition to the young Jesus movement. Saul's activities caused suffering, fear, and death in the Christian community. Although he was sincere in his frenzied opposition, he was very wrong. All of that changed when he encountered Jesus on the Damascus road. As Acts 9 dramatically records, Saul's pride and anger were broken, and he submitted his will to Jesus. The believers' archenemy soon became their most effective spokesman.

The ministry of Saul, better known to us as Paul, would take him on an amazing adventure. Everywhere he went, he told the story of what had happened to him. He became the original missionary, theologian, and church planter. Everyone who has performed those tasks since Paul's time has stood in his shadow.

Paul taught that the Christian faith is incarnational. The mystery of the faith, according to Paul, is "Christ in you, the hope of glory" (Col. 1:27). He spoke of a Christian's body as "a temple of the Holy Spirit" (1 Cor. 6:19). To Paul, salvation involved incarnation—Jesus living within the Christian (see Gal. 2:20). A careful study of Paul's letters reveals that his concern for persons was unlimited. Not only was Paul concerned about winning persons to Christ, but his New Testament letters also reveal his concern for their well-being in every area of life. For example, he very actively raised money to meet the needs of God's people who were experiencing economic problems in Jerusalem (see 1 Cor. 16:1-4).

Evangelism in the first century was never devoid of concern for physical and social needs. The pages of the New Testament burn white-hot with both evangelism and ministry to persons. The miracle of Pentecost resulted in concern for the needy, especially for widows, who had no source of support in that society. Later, when famine spread across the Roman world, the believers in Antioch sent help to the impoverished believers in Judea. The account in Acts says: "The disciples, each according to his ability, decided to provide help for the brothers living in Judea. This they did, sending their gift to the elders by Barnabas and Saul" (Acts 11:29-30). The disciples in Antioch were likely also affected by the famine. Most of them were probably very poor. Yet they had the compassion to reach out in ministry to those in need.

When James wrote his epistle sometime around A.D. 50, he made clear the relationship between concern for those in need and true religion: "Religion that God our Father accepts as pure and faultless is this: to look after orphans and widows in their distress and to keep oneself from being polluted by the world" (Jas. 1:27). Concern and love for others composed what was known as the royal law: "If you keep the royal law found in Scripture, 'Love your neighbor as yourself,' you are doing right" (Jas. 2:8). This royal law echoed Jesus' words (see Matt. 19:19).

In summary, the New Testament writers called believers to—
• live worthy of their calling;
• bear witness of the salvation found only in Jesus Christ;
• relate to fellow Christians and all others in love and service.
Paul summed up his expectation for believers: "As we have opportunity, let us do good to all people, especially to those who belong to the family of believers" (Gal. 6:10). Holy living, witnessing, and serving others were the norm for these Christians.

MINISTRY AND EVANGELISM AFTER THE NEW TESTAMENT ERA

Immediately after the New Testament era the church continued to emphasize and practice evangelism that was characterized by love for persons. Tertullian, one of the early church fathers, described the reputation of the Christians of Carthage in the second century: "It is our care for the helpless, our practice of loving-kindness that brands us in the eyes of our opponents."[4] Celsus wrote of the second-century Christians in Alexandria, "Christians were attracting only worthless and contemptible people, idiots, slaves, poor women, and children."[5] These early believers had a profound sense of mission and destiny that turned the world upside down. They outlived and outloved their enemies. In the words of Adolf Harnack, "The new language on the lips of Christians was the language of love. But it was more than a language, it was a thing of power and action."[6]

Sadly, the fervor that characterized the earliest church and led believers to evangelize and minister cooled and waned over time. Some persons always held high the banner of evangelism and personal ministry; but increasingly, the church neglected the kind of ministry Jesus and the early church emphasized. Several factors probably influenced this demise, the first being doctrinal.

Gnosticism. Heresy invaded the church early in its history. The New Testament suggests the beginnings of gnosticism when the apostle John warned that "many false prophets have gone out into the world" (1 John 4:1). He identified the heresy of these false teachers: "Every spirit that confesseth not that Jesus Christ is come in the flesh is not of God: and this is that spirit of antichrist" (1 John 4:3, KJV). Later, the gnostic heresy would become a full-blown threat to the church's existence.

What does a theological issue such as gnosticism have to do with evangelism and ministry? The Christian gospel is incarnational. Jesus was born not in a palace but in a barn. The smells of animals attended His birth as the peasant girl Mary held Him to her breast. Whatever God's reasons were for sending His Son into such desperately poor circumstances, one of them must have been identification with hurting, struggling persons. Significantly, most of Jesus' earliest followers were among the poor, less advantaged class. As His closest followers He chose Galileans, who were generally disparaged in the Jewish society of that time. Jesus Himself was disparaged by a man who later became a loyal follower. When Philip excitedly told Nathaniel about Jesus, Nathaniel questioned, " 'Nazareth! Can anything good come from there?' " (John 1:46).

Jesus' upbringing was as humble as His birth. Surely, not much could be expected from a person so low on the social scale. Yet His poverty and lowliness were deliberate: "You know the grace of our Lord Jesus Christ, that though He was rich, yet for your sakes he became poor, so that you through his poverty might become rich" (2 Cor. 8:9). Multitudes in that day, as in ours, struggled in abject poverty. Most persons, then as now, lived their lives in ordinary ways. God's heart is always with the masses of hurting people, as He proved by sending His Son in human flesh and into lowly circumstances.

Gnosticism, on the other hand, denied Jesus' true humanity. The thought that Jesus actually came in the flesh was an affront to these heretics. Gnostics were elitists, believing that being human was a curse because all flesh was evil. In their eyes, God was not concerned about struggling, sinning humans. They thought His salvation belonged to the elite, who were able to grasp the secret knowledge of humanity's nature. Persons who held such a distorted belief system had no interest in winning ordinary persons to faith in Jesus and, of course, had little interest in relieving human suffering through ministry.

Monasticism. Another factor that influenced the decline of evangelism and ministry was the rise of monasticism. Sensitive believers were offended by the evil of a world tainted by the desires of the flesh and controlled by the power of the devil. Holy men removed themselves from the world by withdrawing from society and living in solitude or in tightly controlled communities.

These holy men were revered as the best examples of Christian piety. One famous recluse was Simeon Stylites, who climbed to a high cliff and remained on the rock for 37 years. Simeon stood for a year on one foot. He was also famous for being able to touch his head to his toes. Since he lived outdoors, he was filthy and covered with worms; yet people revered him. Sometimes they climbed to the cliff to seek his wisdom, but he never came down. When he died, he was found tied to a post in a posture of prayer. His body was brought down and taken to Antioch, where his funeral procession included 6 bishops, 21 noblemen, and 6,000 soldiers.

Simeon, often called the Great Wonder of the World, was only one of many eccentrics who sought to live a holy life through self-inflicted punishment. A man named Macarius lay naked in a swamp for six months so that mosquitoes and other insects could torment him. Sabrinus would eat only rotted corn to punish his flesh. Others wore iron collars and lived in caves, cemeteries, and dried-up wells. Arsenus wept so profusely over the sins of the world that his eyelashes fell off. All of these and many others sought to serve God by withdrawing from the world and by despising their human frailties.[7]

No one can dispute the dedication of these monastics, nor can we deny their contribution to preserving the best scholarship. Yet withdrawal from the world of sin and struggle is a far cry from the hands-on approach of Jesus and the early church. Jesus walked the roads of human suffering and sin. He touched the untouchables and associated with the least desirable persons in society. When He prayed for His followers, He said, " 'My prayer is not that you take them out of the world but that you protect them from the evil one' " (John 17:15). Mystics and comtemplatives may have held roles in church history, but withdrawal from the world is not true to Jesus' example. Christians must find their arena of ministry in the real world with all its sin.

Although no exact parallel to monasticism exists in evangelical circles today, Christians may nonetheless hide behind the church building's protective walls. This kind of siege mentality sees the real world as the enemy of piety and separation from the world as the highest expression of faith. To such Christians, the church is a fortress from a dangerous world. Good Christians study the Bible, lead moral lives, and participate in church activities. An old saying claims that a person must be physically strong to be a Baptist, meaning that much strength is required just to attend all of the church meetings, serve on the committees, and fill all of the positions in the church's organizations. An unfortunate reality is that a person can use church activities to avoid a hurting world. Church activities are important but only as a means to carry out ministry in the world. Keeping church members occupied with the organized church may cause them to feel that they are living effective Christian lives; but if we use the church as an escape from the real world, we miss the point. Christians are not called to be monastics, seeking to escape a wicked, corrupt world. Our place of service is ultimately in the world, not in the church building.

Institutionalization. A third factor that led the church away from its mission of redemptive, incarnational service is the institutionalization of the church. When the Edict of Milan gave legal status to Christianity in A.D. 313, it ceased to be seen as a despised sect. The church experienced further legitimacy when Constantine, a nominal Christian, became the sole emperor of the Roman Empire. These events led masses of people to convert to Christianity. When Theodosius proclaimed Christianity the state religion of the Roman Empire in A.D. 380, the church was given official status. This made becoming a Christian the acceptable thing to do; but according to Findley B. Edge, this "led away from the idea of a regenerate church membership and led eventually toward institutionalism in religion."[8]

Once religion becomes institutionalized, its fire tends to die. The focus then becomes the preservation of the institution. The history of the Christian church from the fourth century until the Reformation reflects a growing institutionalism. The institutional church became rich and powerful. Creedalism and ecclesiasticism replaced concern for individuals. In fact, the individual existed to serve and strengthen the institution rather than the church's existing to evangelize and minister to individuals. Church leaders became masters instead of servants. Religion majored on adherence to accepted dogma and ceremony. In the words of Findley B. Edge, "The individual was held in the strong, cold hand of authoritative ecclesiasticism."[9] Although we can find many notable exceptions to the loss of concern for ministry to the individual during these centuries, the church largely functioned as an institution, concerned mainly with its own preservation.

Gnosticism, monasticism, and institutionalization left the church with little concern for persons' physical or spiritual needs. Persons were seen as existing to enrich the institution. Bishops and clerics took care of spiritual matters, having little direct involvement with persons.

MINISTRY AND EVANGELISM IN THE REFORMATION PERIOD

A mighty, fresh wind began to blow on the institutional church through the influence of men such as John Wycliffe and John Huss. These and others who sought to restore evangelical life to the church were cruelly suppressed by an all-powerful church, but what they started could not be imprisoned behind the dark walls of institutionalism. The 16th century saw Martin Luther and those who followed him strike a mighty blow at the impersonal, institutional church. We call their movement the Protestant Reformation. The principles of the Reformation called Christians back to the New Testament emphasis on justification by faith, the authority of the

Scriptures, and the priesthood of believers. According to these principles, salvation was a matter of individual response to the gospel, not something that could be granted or taken away by the church. Because every Christian is a priest, ordinary Christians could read, study, and interpret the Bible. The believer's priesthood also meant that ministry to those within and outside the church was every believer's job.

Sadly, the reformers, even Luther, became authoritative and intolerant of opposing views. Some victories of the Reformation did not survive long, especially the idea that every believer is a priest. The human tendency to creedalize and institutionalize almost always appears. Soon powerful state churches once again lost the fervor of individual salvation and ministry.

Although many gains of the Reformation seemed lost, God raised up persons who insisted on worshiping Him according to the dictates of their consciences. These brave Christians could not be contained in yet another institutional church. Many suffered, and some died; but from their commitment to principle came the free-church movement—a far more radical and complete reformation of the church. Baptists are part of that brave tradition.

Two strong theological pillars of Baptist belief are a regenerate church membership and religious liberty. Baptists reject infant baptism, insisting on personal salvation. Baptists also insist on the right of individuals to worship God as each sees fit, with no coercion from the state or from an all-powerful church.[10] From these principles grew an emphasis on the priesthood of every believer. Every Christian is a minister. Every Christian has the right and privilege to proclaim the gospel and minister to persons in Christ's name. As we have seen, this truth is a foundation on which ministry evangelism is built.

THE PLACE OF MINISTRY AND EVANGELISM IN EVANGELICAL AWAKENINGS

Great movements of God, growing from the Reformation and the free-church tradition, have always been accompanied by a quickening of the social conscience. The Great Awakening of the 18th century emphasized passionate preaching and social ministry. During that time John Wesley, the founder of Methodism, taught his followers to minister to the poor, the disadvantaged, and the imprisoned. Wesley influenced much social reform in England, including prison reform. He once said, "The gospel of Christ knows no religion but social, no holiness but social holiness."[11] Wesley's ministry burned with evangelistic fervor, but he maintained an equally strong concern for ministry to persons in need.

Charles Finney is often called the father of modern evangelism. The history of his powerful ministry would justify that title. Yet Finney was also the leading social reformer of his time. Oberlin College, where Finney taught, was known as a hotbed of revivalism and social concern. The mistaken idea that evangelism and social ministry are incompatible, even hostile to each other, does not conform to biblical or historical reality. Clearly, God intended for evangelism to be incarnational; to be concerned for whole persons; and to minister to their bodies, minds, and spirits. Most of the social and humanitarian advances of this century were born in the context of revival. A strong link has always existed between evangelical-Christian fervor and social justice.

The 20th century has brought many changes, positive and negative, to the church. Evangelical churches, including Baptists, have advanced on the socioeconomic scale. Early in their history Baptists, especially in the South, were identified with the less affluent, less educated elements of society. Southern Baptists in particular have experienced tremendous growth in numbers and influence. Since its beginning in 1845 the Southern Baptist Convention has grown to be the largest Protestant denomination in the world. This growth has made it possible for Southern Baptists to become a major force in world missions and evangelism. Southern Baptists, along with other evangelical groups, have moved to the front line of influence in this country. Large buildings, budgets, and memberships have made Baptist and other evangelical churches powerful influences in their communities.

Some persons have recently wondered whether our prosperity has dimmed our vision for ministry. If so, the commitment to caring ministry has suffered most. A church can be so intent on growth that it forgets its call to minister to the sinful, broken, and impoverished, as well as to the attractive, affluent, and powerful.

This brief historical sketch has illustrated the ease with which a church can lose the sharp focus on incarnational ministry that reaches out to those who are hurting. A small church in a midwestern town was the chief beneficiary of a very wealthy woman's will. After the estate was settled, the church became the wealthiest congregation in town. However, it had one serious problem: the church members could not agree on what to do with the money. Quarrels over the money caused some members to leave the church. Others remained to ensure that the money was used wisely. The shrinking congregation now exists behind the protective walls of the little sanctuary. The church has lost its vision and its sense of mission. Its main priority now seems to be holding on to its wealth. This true story may serve as a parable of what happens to any congregation when it turns inward, making self-preservation its main business.

Incarnational evangelism may once again be under attack. The church's true mission, to be Christ's body in the world, may be thwarted by a new kind of gnosticism that makes the gospel elitist, separating it from the flesh and blood of real life. Through a new monasticism the gospel, given as good news to a sin-filled world, may be diverted to a message of escape from the world under the guise of separation from the world. Or God's redemptive purpose for all people may be interrupted as the church turns inward to self-preservation through deadly institutionalism. All of these errors deny incarnational evangelism that involves itself with persons in their hurts and pain, just as Christ took on human flesh and lived in the world of human sin and weakness. The church must overcome these errors if it is to carry out the biblical mandates to witness and minister.

EVANGELISM AS IT WAS MEANT TO BE

In *Conspiracy of Kindness* Steve Sjogren quotes Rebecca Pippert's observation: "Christians and non-Christians have one thing in common: They both hate evangelism."[12] While this may be a bit of an overstatement, it contains a measure of truth. Christians do not hate evangelism, but they fear it. Most believers are thrilled when another person accepts Jesus Christ and begins to follow Him. Most also understand that someone must be willing to do the work of evangelism. Many, if not most, Christians want God to use them to bring others to Christ. The problem is that Christian leaders often expect believers to witness when they do not feel capable of doing so. This problem leads to serious frustration for many sincere believers. What Christian has not heard a pastor bring a stirring message about the responsibility of every believer to win others to Christ and made a well-intentioned vow to accept that challenge? But many, after making an awkward effort or two, have given up on the task. Many have concluded that evangelism is for the pros, not for ordinary Christians. Of course, nothing could be farther from the truth. Every person who knows Jesus Christ has the responsibility and privilege of bringing others to Him.

Sjogren writes that his attempts to share the gospel can be divided into three phases: the shark, the carp, and the dolphin. The shark phase pictures aggressive, confrontational evangelism, which is the picture most persons have of an evangelistic witness: someone who is loud, pushy, opinionated, and perhaps angry. The shark is always trying to move in for the kill. Persons are souls to be won. Not much attention is given to the whole person's needs and hurts. Many times zealous, young-in-the-faith believers are sharks. Their desire to win others is admirable, but confrontation sometimes alienates more persons than it wins. Christians who approach witnessing this way are likely to become discouraged and to quit trying. Most of us are just not cut out to be high-pressure salespersons, and most persons do not appreciate this approach, even though we are trying to sell the gospel.

The carp phase of evangelism is the opposite of the shark phase. Carp swim on the bottom of the river and live on what other fish discard. Unlike sharks, they are passive and lethargic. Carp do not attack at all but just watch the world go by. Many Christians are like carp when it comes to witnessing: they just don't do it! Some of these lethargic believers were formerly sharks, having tried aggressive witnessing. Perhaps they even learned a high-pressure method to make persons pray a prayer or make a decision. But because their confrontational approach offended others, they got tired of being rebuffed and quit witnessing except with their daily lives. When carp are challenged by a pastor or an evangelist to win others to Christ, they take it with a grain of salt. Many of these persons are active church members but have opted out of personal evangelism.

Sjogren identifies the third phase or style of evangelism as the dolphin stage. Dolphins combine the strengths of sharks and carp. They move through the water effectively and with purpose, but they have fun doing it. They are not aggressive like the shark, nor are they listless like the carp. Dolphin-style Christians are deeply committed to evangelism; but they evangelize in a relational, natural way. This kind of evangelism attracts rather than repels. It is incarnational in its nature and approach.[13]

Although we might not choose any of these categories to describe our attitude toward witnessing, all of us find ourselves somewhere on a continuum when it comes to evangelism. At the high end of the continuum are believers who regularly make efforts to bring others to Christ. At the low end are those who make no effort at all. Many Christians find themselves somewhere between these two points. They know the importance of the Great Commission. They understand that winning persons to faith in Jesus Christ is not optional. The question is how they are to go about this task. The best answer to that question is incarnational evangelism—words that become flesh.

Incarnational evangelism involves both words and deeds. Elton Trueblood reminds us: "Testimony must be both deed and word. The spoken word is never really effective unless it is backed up by a life, but it is also true that the living deed is never adequate without the support which the spoken word can provide. This is because no life is ever good enough. The person who says naively, 'I don't need to preach; I just let my life speak,' is insufferably self-righteous. What one among us is so good that he can let his life speak and leave it at that?"[14]

Incarnational evangelism, referred to as ministry evangelism at First Baptist Church, Leesburg, Florida, combines word and deed. This kind of evangelism demonstrates Christ's love by unconditionally ministering to persons at the point of their need, hurt, or brokenness. Then the person is confronted with the claims of Christ in an effort to lead the person to accept Him as Savior and to follow Him as Lord. Ministry evangelism takes seriously the words of E. Stanley Jones: "The social gospel divorced from personal salvation is like a body without a soul; the message of personal salvation without a social dimension is like a soul without a body. The former is a corpse, the latter is a ghost."[15]

Evangelism and social ministry are not mutually exclusive, although many persons have thought that this is the case. The church does not have to choose one to the exclusion or diminishment of the other. Incarnational evangelism is show and tell. Christ's love is shown in deeds of kindness and ministry. Christ's message is shared as the reason for it all. Christ's redemptive purpose for each individual is the goal. Ministry evangelism is based on a holistic view of persons—the biblical view of the unity of the spiritual and physical fused together as a living soul (see Gen. 2:7). This view rejects a dualistic view of humans, which emphasizes spiritual redemption while neglecting physical and social needs. On the other hand, ministry evangelism rejects the idea that meeting physical and social needs alone meets persons' deepest needs.

First Baptist Church in Leesburg, Florida, operates on the premise that the gospel must be taken out of the air-conditioned comfort of the worship center and into the lives of empty, hurting persons. When the ministry approach to evangelism is criticized, Pastor Charles Roesel responds: "It is not a kind of social gospel or rice-bowl Christianity. We are there to love persons and to minister to them. Even if they do not make a decision for Christ, we are still going to minister to them. We want to do more than just minister to the physical needs they have. We want them to know Jesus. The only way they can have eternal peace and joy is through Him. We see no conflict at all in meeting human needs and the real need of their soul."

While First Baptist Church, Leesburg, serves as an example of how persons can be reached for Christ through caring ministry, every church and every Christian can practice ministry evangelism. Even a small church with limited resources can discover areas of human hurt and need to which they can respond. It is not necessary to begin with a large or costly program. First Baptist, Leesburg, started with only one ministry. Ministry evangelism is not another program to be added to the many programs and activities of already busy congregations. Ministry evangelism is a way of looking at a church's work. It views the purpose of the church as giving itself away in loving service and faithful witness. When we are willing to become Christ's ministers to broken persons, God honors our witness and provides resources for our ministry.

Anita Cross, who sought help in the Women's Shelter in Leesburg with her six-year-old daughter, said: "This is a place to get myself together. Most women stay in a bad place because they don't have any place to go." Then Anita added, "I just thank God First Baptist has this ministry."[16]

A member of First Baptist, Leesburg, wrote a poem titled "How Shall I Feed Them?"

> I was well fed,
> So I did not see the hungry child standing next to me.
> Nor did I see the look of fear in the young mother's eyes
> As she held the child near.
> I had the means within my grasp.
> I thought nothing of the anxious clasp of the old man's hands
> As he faced a debt and thought of the funds he could not get.
> I was not in bonds; I was free,
> So I could self-righteously pass by the jail,
> For I was good and did the things that a Christian should.
> Yes, I went to Sunday School and church,
> And I could turn my head from the stumbling lurch of the
>   drunken man
> As he fell in the gutter with a burden so great he could not utter it.
> And so I went along my way, saw nothing but a sun-filled day,
> And did good deeds.
> I failed to see the very ones who needed me,
> And when at last it was time for bed,
> Dutifully, my prayers I said.
> I tried in vain to go to sleep,
> But a voice said sharply, "Feed My sheep!"
> I heard someone call my name, and slowly to my vision
> Came the child and the mother, hand in hand,
> The frightened face of the tired old man,
> The prison and the souls inside,
> And the drunken man in the gutter.
> I said: "O Lord, how can this be?

There were too many here for me."
And He replied gently,
"There is a way
With sufficiency to meet your day.
This is how it can be done:
You can feed them one by one."[17]

Ministry evangelism is about caring. It is about giving desperate and needy persons a loving touch. But it is caring with a difference. That difference is Jesus—the reason for it all.

---

[1]Lesley Clark, "Christian Care Village to Help Those in Need," *The Lake Sentinel*, 20 February 1994, 8, col. 4.
[2]Findley B. Edge, *The Doctrine of the Laity* (Nashville: Convention Press, 1985), 52.
[3]Findley B. Edge, *A Quest for Vitality in Religion* (Nashville: Broadman Press, 1963), 85.
[4]Thomas S. Rainer, ed., *Evangelism in the 21st Century* (Wheaton: Harold Shaw Publishers, 1989), 11.
[5]Ibid., 12.
[6]Adolf Harnack, *The Mission and Expansion of Christianity in the First Three Centuries*, vol. 1 (New York: Harper & Row, 1908), 149.
[7]Frank S. Mead, *Rebels with a Cause* (Nashville: Abingdon Press, 1964), 58–61.
[8]Edge, *A Quest for Vitality in Religion*, 53.
[9]Ibid., 56.
[10]Ibid., 62.
[11]Edge, *The Doctrine of the Laity*, 69.
[12]Adapted from *Conspiracy of Kindness*, © copyright 1993 by Steve Sjogren. Published by Servant Publications, Box 8617, Ann Arbor, Michigan 48107. Used by permission.
[13]Ibid., 34–41.
[14]Elton Trueblood, *The Company of the Committed* (New York: Harper and Row, 1961), 53.
[15]Thomas S. Rainer, ed., *Evangelism in the 21st Century*, 19.
[16]Clark, "Christian Care Village to Help Those in Need," 8, col. 5.
[17]Used by permission of the poet, who wishes to remain anonymous.

2

God and Hurting Persons

I THOUGHT THE DAY would never end! A transient family—a man, a woman, and three small children—was in the church parking lot when I arrived at my office before 8:00 a.m. Their story was a familiar one. They had been on their way home to a distant state when their automobile broke down. They had no money for repairs, food, and lodging. The story seemed legitimate, and the need was obvious. The plight of the children, especially—poorly dressed, confused, and frightened—tugged at my heart. I spent several hours trying to find help for them. By using church resources, calling on businesspersons, and contributing my own money, I was able to meet their immediate needs for food and shelter and to arrange for the family to get home. When I left them at the motel, I prayed with them and assured them of God's love.

When I finally got to my office, I was exhausted and even a little resentful. I had planned for a busy day in my study. Now I had neither time nor energy to do the work I had hoped to do. The hours-long interruption necessitated by that one needy family had made a shambles of my schedule. I decided to salvage what was left of my day by simply being still and trying to regain my physical and spiritual composure. As I began reading in Proverbs, verse 17 of chapter 19 made its way straight to my heart:

> He who is kind to the poor lends to the Lord,
>   and he will reward him for what he has done.

This became a teachable moment for me, as though God had spoken directly and personally: "Your day has not been wasted, as you imagined. When you took time to help that needy family, you were actually serving Me. What you and your congregation gave to them was really like a loan to Me." I knew that the loan would not necessarily be repaid in dollars and cents. Instead, I learned that God's heart is with the needy. When we help such persons, we are doing His work. In His own way and time He will "reward" or bless those who join Him in this service.

The truth expressed in Proverbs 19:17 is often repeated in Scripture. Jesus' words recorded in Matthew 25:31-45 powerfully affirm that ministry to persons in need is, in reality, service to the Lord. Later in this chapter we will study this passage in more detail. For now we will capture its basic thrust. The passage paints a picture of the final judgment. As persons stand before Christ in judgment, they are divided into two groups as a shepherd would divide the sheep from the goats. Those on Christ's right hand, the sheep, are commended for ministering to the Lord when He was hungry, thirsty, lonely, sick, and imprisoned. Yet these righteous ones respond that they cannot recall seeing the Lord with these needs or how they met them. The response of Christ, the King, is " 'Whatever you did for one of the least of these brothers of mine, you did for me' " (Matt. 25:40). The truth emerges that Christ regards very seriously the needs of hurting persons. As a matter of fact, He so closely identifies Himself with hurting persons that meeting their needs is tantamount to meeting His needs.

A smug and erroneous idea often expressed in religious circles is that if persons are poor, disadvantaged, oppressed, and needy, they are products of their own choices and therefore have received what they deserve. We often dismiss such persons as lazy, unwilling to help themselves, and unworthy of sympathy. We are especially vulnerable to this attitude when we are full, employed, and healthy.

We all know that some persons live on public assistance or go from one organization or church to another seeking a handout. Unfortunately, we permit these persons to influence our thinking so much that we generalize, concluding that all need and pain exist because these persons will not work and help themselves. This attitude is not only judgmental and unfair but also unbiblical and clearly unchristian. God has great compassion for the hurting and needy. Since He is a God of love and grace, He is concerned even for those whose sin and lack of character have caused their suffering. Therefore, even if persons' actions have led to their pain, we are not free to dismiss them as lazy, depraved, or unworthy. After all, who among us really deserves God's grace and love?

GOD'S COMPASSION FOR HURTING PERSONS

A serious study of Scripture reveals the truth that God is deeply concerned with persons' needs, especially persons who are poor, needy, or oppressed. Theology is by definition a study of God. Such a study is always a bit presumptuous. As mortals, with all of our limitations, we are capable of knowing about God only what He chooses to reveal to us. God spoke powerfully through the prophet Isaiah the truth that we mortals cannot comprehend the eternal mystery of His being:

> "My thoughts are not your thoughts,
>   neither are your ways my ways," declares the Lord.
> "As the heavens are higher than the earth,
>   so are my ways higher than your ways
>   and my thoughts than your thoughts" (Isa. 55:8-9).

When Job struggled to make sense of the sorrow, suffering, and complexity that had turned his life upside down, he found no answers in his friends' judgmental advice or in his own reasoning processes. God addressed Job's situation in the latter part of the ancient book that bears Job's name. The magnificent poetry of Job 38—41 is unsurpassed in biblical literature. In substance God reminded Job that he, Job, was mortal and therefore not fully aware of God's eternal ways. Job would not be able to solve the problem of his suffering because he was finite. So much he did not know and could not know. When God reminded Job of His creative power and unfailing purpose, Job was humbled to the dust:

> Then Job replied to the Lord:
> "I know that you can do all things;
>   no plan of yours can be thwarted.
> You asked, 'Who is this that obscures my counsel without
>   knowledge?'
> Surely I spoke of things I did not understand,
>   things too wonderful for me to know" (Job 42:1-3).

The lesson Job learned is one that all who attempt to speak of God in any defining way would do well to heed. Whenever we speak of God, we must confess,

> "Surely I spoke of things I did not understand,
>   things too wonderful for me to know" (Job 42:3).

The apostle Paul gave witness to the same truth about the mystery that surrounds God and our inability to understand or explain His nature and actions fully. As he concluded a long, somewhat complicated discussion of God's saving actions toward Jews and Gentiles (Rom. 9—11), he seems to have come to the end of logic and reason; so he simply concluded by breaking into a doxology of praise:

> Oh, the depth of the riches of the wisdom and knowledge
> of God!
> How unsearchable his judgments,
> and his paths beyond tracing out!
> "Who has known the mind of the Lord?
> Or who has been his counselor?"
> "Who has ever given to God,
> that God should repay him?"
> For from him and through him and to him are all things.
> To him be the glory forever!
> Amen (Rom. 11:33-36).

Like Job and so many who have been confronted by God's mystery and majesty, Paul was driven to an attitude of worship and awe before God, whose judgments are unsearchable and whose paths are beyond tracing.

The truth that God is God and therefore beyond our human ability to understand fully should always guard us from making rash statements about His character and attributes. Theology must always be approached from the vantage point of humility and a confession that "we know in part and we prophesy in part" (1 Cor. 13:9). Actually, we know about God only what He has chosen to tell us. This is the reason we speak of revelation. The Christian faith is based on the fact that God has chosen to reveal Himself to us. Therefore, what we believe about God does not grow from our own hopes and intuitions, no matter how noble. We know God only as He chooses to make Himself known to us. God has made that choice. Through holy Scripture and especially through Jesus, God has told us a lot about Himself (see Heb. 1:1-3).

We know, for example, that God is the Creator (see Gen 1:1). Because He created everything that exists, He owns it all:

> The earth is the Lord's, and everything in it,
> the world, and all who live in it (Ps. 24:1).

God's creative activity illustrates one of His attributes, His almighty power. In the words of the psalmist,

> Great is our Lord and mighty in power (Ps. 147:5).

The almighty God is also holy. His holiness is absolute. No taint of sin is present in His nature. The writer of Exodus described His holiness in powerful words:

> "Who among the gods is like you, O Lord?
> Who is like you—
>   majestic in holiness,
>   awesome in glory,
>   working wonders?" (Ex. 15:11).

The New Testament, especially, lifts up the most amazing attribute of God. John wrote, "God is love" (1 John 4:8). This amazing verse is one of the few statements in the Bible that attempt to define God. God is, in His very essence, love. This truth is important because it leads us to begin to understand how He relates to persons. Someone can affirm that God is almighty and holy yet still think of Him as removed from the daily struggles of human life, unconcerned about human hurts and needs. But the fact that God is love clearly implies that He cares about persons. He wants to redeem them, and He involves Himself in their struggles. This revealed truth about God's character, nature, and attitude serves as the foundation on which ministry evangelism is built. Because God loves persons and cares for their needs, we are to love them, minister to them, and witness to them of His love.

GOD'S CARE IN THE OLD TESTAMENT

The writer of Psalm 145 gave an eloquent testimony to God's mercy toward His creation:

> Your kingdom is an everlasting kingdom,
>   and your dominion endures through all generations.
> The Lord is faithful to all his promises
>   and loving toward all he has made.
> The Lord upholds all those who fall
>   and lifts up all who are bowed down.
> The eyes of all look to you,
>   and you give them their food at the proper time.
> You open your hand
>   and satisfy the desires of every living thing (Ps. 145:13-17).

This poem to God's mercy includes several key ideas reflecting the way

God relates to persons. For example, God is "loving toward all He has made" (v. 13). God's loving care for persons has its roots in creation. This love can be observed in the fact that He created humans. Scripture reveals that Adam and Eve were made in His image (see Gen. 1:27). This is not said of anything else God created. Only humans were made to be like God, to relate to Him, and to have fellowship with Him. From the beginning God demonstrated great care for the man He made. Adam's loneliness concerned his Maker, so God created a companion, a woman, for him (see Gen. 2:18). God understood the human need for meaningful and fulfilling work, so He gave him the garden of Eden to tend (see Gen. 2:15). The Creator was concerned that humans have wholesome food to eat, so He gave them food-producing plants for their use (see Gen. 1:29). Then when man and woman lost their innocence, God clothed them to cover their nakedness (see Gen. 3:21). Even when Cain killed his brother, Abel, God was concerned about Cain's fear of being hunted down and killed. Therefore, He put a seal of protection on him (see Gen. 4:13-15). These examples provide evidence that God has been concerned about persons' most basic needs from the very beginning.

The psalmist continued his affirmation of God's mercy:

> The Lord upholds all those who fall
> and lifts up all those who are bowed down (Ps. 145:14).

The Old Testament offers many examples of God's concern for a person who is fearful or in trouble. When Abram took matters into his own hands to father a son, he slept with his wife's maid, Hagar, who became pregnant by him. Although the whole arrangement was originally Sarai's idea, she found herself despising the woman who could give Abram what she seemed unable to give him—a son. Sarai mistreated Hagar and caused her so much pain that she ran away (see Gen. 16:1-6).

Hagar's situation was desperate. She was frightened, alone, and without recourse because she was only a slave. Somewhere in her lonely journey "the angel of the Lord found Hagar" (Gen. 16:7), ministered to her, and gave her God's promise about the child she would bear. Hagar gave God an unusual but meaningful name that day: " 'You are the God who sees me' " (v. 13). The name Hagar gave to the Lord literally means "the well of the living one who sees." Then she explained, " 'I have now seen the One who sees me' " (v. 13). What a beautiful tribute! And what a testimony to God, who comes to the aid of the powerless and despairing!

The writer of Psalm 145 further stated,

> The eyes of all look to you,
>> and you give them their food at the proper time (Ps. 145:15).

This is a confession of absolute dependence on God's provision and wonderful assurance that He desires to provide for our most basic needs.

As if to sum up all he had written to assure us of God's concern and care for humans, the writer said of God, "You open your hand" (Ps. 145:16). There have always been persons to whom every door and hand seem closed. But to the poor, the weak, the alienated, and the powerless, God holds out an open hand of love.

Many other Old Testament passages describe or assure us of God's caring love for all persons. The Psalms are especially rich with such assurances. For example, Psalm 25 addresses God: "Remember, O Lord, thy tender mercies and thy loving-kindnesses, for they have been ever of old" (Ps. 25:6, KJV). The Old Testament concept of God's loving-kindness (*hessed*) is the equivalent of the New Testament concept of God's grace (*charis*). Both of these terms relate to God's love in action toward humankind.

Similar truth about God is expressed in Psalm 100:

> The Lord is good and his love endures forever;
>> his faithfulness continues through all generations
>>> (Ps. 100:5).

The words of Psalm 145 are also powerful:

> The Lord is gracious and compassionate,
>> slow to anger and rich in love.
> The Lord is good to all;
>> he has compassion on all he has made (Ps. 145:8-9).

The consistent picture of God that emerges in the Old Testament is one of love, concern, provision, and redemption. With all His power and holiness God is best understood by His love. This love extends to all creation, especially to humans, made in His image.

GOD'S PEOPLE AND CARING MINISTRY

Not only is the Lord God compassionate toward all, especially those in need, but He also made clear from the beginning that He expects His people to be compassionate toward others. As Moses led the Israelites toward the promised land, God gave the laws by which He expected His people to live. Much of the covenant between God and His people related to personal morality and correct religious practice. But Scripture makes clear that God expected His covenant people to treat others as He treated them.

Reminding the people of their responsibility to reverence and love the Lord, Moses pointed out that God "defends the cause of the fatherless and the widow, and loves the alien, giving him food and clothing. And you are to love those who are aliens, for you yourself were aliens in Egypt" (Deut. 10:18-19). In His mercy "He Himself takes the part of those who have no civil rights of their own."[1] Not long before, the children of Israel had been slaves in Egypt, burdened with heavy workloads under Pharaoh's cruel hand. They had never been able to satisfy their cruel taskmasters and had enjoyed no rights. They had endured humiliation and suffering, and many had died. Surely, the memory of their suffering and of God's merciful deliverance would serve to make them compassionate to others who were suffering. Unfortunately, we soon forget how much we needed mercy and how good God has been to us when we are confronted with others who are hurting. God warned His people to avoid this tragic, mistaken attitude.

Israel's care for the poor and downtrodden was to be expressed in very specific ways. The Lord commanded: " 'When you reap the harvest of your land, do not reap to the very edges of your field or gather the gleanings of your harvest. Do not go over your vineyard a second time or pick up the grapes that have fallen. Leave them for the poor and the alien. I am the Lord your God' " (Lev. 19:9-10). The pagan practice of leaving the fields ungleaned was pre-Israelite. From ancient times grain or fruit was left in the fields for what the people imagined to be the spirits of the field. God's command had a different purpose—a humanitarian one.[2] God wanted His people to be concerned with the needs of the poor and of the stranger who had no land and no power. We need not make too much of the fact that the needy got only the leftovers. The point is that God wanted His people to provide for the poor. Leaving the fields ungleaned would provide food— the difference between life and death for many.

God's directives to care for the needs of the downtrodden and poor are consistent with His nature and character. He is always on the side of the oppressed and disadvantaged. His heart is always with the struggler. Study of both the Old and New Testaments confirms that aspect of His purpose and nature.

THE PROPHETS AND GOD'S CONCERN FOR PERSONS
The popular understanding of prophecy focuses on the ability to predict

the future. Although the Old Testament prophets often spoke of things yet to come, they majored on the task of speaking God's Word to the people of their own time. Robert N. Sanders defines *prophet* as someone "who stood within the historical framework of his own day and time and spoke for God by seeking to interpret the divine will to men."[3] This understanding of the Old Testament prophets is strongly supported by the powerful messages they spoke to the people of their times.

One recurring theme of the prophets was social justice. This is especially true of the prophets we refer to as the eighth-century-B.C. prophets—Amos, Hosea, Isaiah, and Micah. The eighth century B.C. was a time of prosperity and apparent peace in Israel and Judah. The defeat of the Syrians, who had subjected Israel to fierce tyranny, brought a new day to both the northern and southern kingdoms. The Assyrians had defeated the Syrians but were unable to occupy Palestine. For about 65 years, from 805 to 740 B.C., the land enjoyed peace. When Jeroboam II came to power in Israel in 783 B.C., he began a vigorous program of military and economic development. In the south Uzziah enjoyed similar success. This became a period of expansion, freedom, peace, and prosperity. The powerful people of both kingdoms thought their prosperity would never end.[4]

In the midst of optimism and plenty, cancerous problems ate away the life of the two nations. Self-indulgence, pride, idolatry, and immorality were rampant. A gap widened between the rich and the poor. The poor were often driven from their land and were forced to crowd into the cities, where their situations worsened. Widespread oppression and enslavement afflicted the poor. Most tragic of all, the prosperous and powerful had little concern for the needs of these hurting and powerless persons.

God's heart is always with suffering persons. His judgment always eventually falls on those who injure, oppress, and ignore those who are needy and hurting. Into the extravagant, prideful optimism of that time, God sent His prophets with messages of warning and pleas for the oppressed. These men—Amos and Hosea in Israel, Isaiah and Micah in Judah—were powerful messengers. They could not be ignored, even though history proves that their warnings were largely unheeded. For the purposes of this study we will limit our examination of their messages to their words about the treatment of the poor and powerless.

Today's sins toward oppressed persons usually take the form of ignoring them and failing to reach out to them in ministry and evangelism. The problems the prophets addressed were worse. In that time the prosperous beat down and even enslaved the poor and needy. Although the situation is different, the principle is the same: God loves hurting persons, and He expects those who claim to love Him to reach out to them with redemptive love.

Amos is one of the most colorful and heroic figures in the pages of Scripture. He did not come from a long line of prophets or religious leaders. Rather, he was a simple countryman from a small village near Jerusalem. In the village of Tekoa Amos tended sheep and took care of sycamore-fig trees. From this humble setting God called Amos and commissioned him to go to Israel with His message (see Amos 7:14-15).

When Amos arrived in Israel, he observed unprecedented prosperity. Business was good. Wine was flowing freely. In fact, the rich were drinking it by the bowlful (see Amos 6:6). The affluent lived in fine houses that had the best furnishings. They ate the most expensive food and enjoyed the pleasures of the good life (see Amos 6:4-5).

In the midst of this affluence the poor were being trampled. When Amos appeared in Samaria to deliver God's message, his starting point was the treatment of the poor:

> "For three sins of Israel,
>   even for four, I will not turn back my wrath.
> They sell the righteous for silver,
>   and the needy for a pair of sandals.
> They trample on the heads of the poor
>   as upon the dust of the ground
>   and deny justice to the oppressed" (Amos 2:6-7).

This theme, introduced early in Amos' message, fills the remainder of his prophecy. Even the wealthy women, referred to as "cows of Bashan ... who oppress the poor and crush the needy," were soundly condemned for their treatment of those less fortunate (Amos 4:1). In the midst of plenty the people were arrogant, self-centered, self-indulgent, and callous to the poor and oppressed.

Perhaps the most plaintive accusation Amos leveled at the rich populace was that in the enjoyment of their plenty, they did not care. Amos said of them, "You do not grieve over the ruin of Joseph" (Amos 6:6). They had all they wanted and thought it would never end. It did not matter to them that the disadvantaged were being left out of the bountiful wealth. As with Pharaoh's enslavement of the children of Israel centuries earlier, Joseph's people were being ruined. In the words of Robert Sanders, "Everywhere Amos saw evidence of this cleavage between those who lived in opulence and idleness and those shackled by the chains of poverty."[5]

The point that must not be missed is that God sent His prophet to speak out for the poor: "Amos' prophetic burden was directed toward that kind of religion which is no longer able to identify with the weak, the poor, and the dispossessed."[6] In many ways our society resembles Israel of the eighth century B.C. We live in an affluent environment, but evangelical Christianity seldom addresses the gap between the haves and the have-nots. Like the religious people of Amos's time, we are often oblivious to the need and pain around us. But we can be certain that the God who sent Amos to prophesy to Israel understands and cares about the needy.

The indifference of those who claimed to love God toward those who were poor is a recurring theme in the writings of the other prophets of the eighth century B.C. Micah cried out against those who—

> covet fields and seize them,
>   and houses, and take them.
> They defraud a man of his home,
>   a fellowman of his inheritance (Mic. 2:2).

The oppression of the poor did not stop with ignoring their needs. The affluent were so callous toward them that they even conspired to take away the little that the poor had, even their humble homes.

Some of the most powerful directives to help the needy are found in the writings of the prophets. God led Isaiah to identify the kind of religious observance that is pleasing to Him:

> "Is not this the kind of fasting I have chosen:
> to loose the chains of injustice
>   and untie the cords of the yoke,
> to set the oppressed free
>   and break every yoke?
> Is it not to share your food with the hungry
>   and to provide the poor wanderer with shelter—
> when you see the naked, to clothe him,
>   and not to turn away from your own flesh and blood?"
>   (Isa. 58:6-7).

True worship of God looses chains of oppression, sets people free, feeds the hungry, gives shelter to the homeless, and clothes the naked.

Micah placed human responsibility to God in direct relationship to justice and mercy:

> He has showed you, O man, what is good.
> And what does the Lord require of you?
> To act justly and to love mercy
> and to walk humbly with your God (Mic. 6:8).

Amos warned the people that God would reject their ritualized worship. He would refuse their offerings and would not listen to their songs (see Amos 5:21-23). Their sin, especially the contempt they felt toward the poor, made their worship unacceptable. What, then, did God require of His people? The prophet spoke with poetic eloquence:

> "Let justice roll on like a river,
> righteousness like a never-failing stream!" (Amos 5:24).

The God of the prophets is the God of eternity. His heart is always with the oppressed. His expectations for those who would serve Him are always justice, compassion, and mercy.

JESUS AND HURTING PERSONS

Because Jesus was God in human flesh, we can expect that His ministry also emphasized compassion for the needy. From time to time throughout Christian history, scholars have made an effort to discover the Jesus of history, raising important questions such as: What was He really like? How did He live? What did He teach? Have centuries of dogma and tradition so distorted our view of Him that we really do not understand Him? Such efforts, however, are doomed to failure unless they are based on the only trustworthy witness—the holy Scriptures, especially the four Gospels. Only scant and inconclusive information is available about Jesus outside the biblical record. Although scholars can better understand that record by studying the place and time in which He lived out His earthly life, they must inevitably turn to the Bible to learn anything substantial about Him.

An effort to understand Jesus is important. People often try to recreate Jesus in their own image. In the words of H. Stephen Shoemaker, we change the words found in the Psalms, "This is the day the Lord has made" (Ps. 118:24), and make them read, "This is the Lord the day has made."[7] In other words, we try to cast Jesus in the mold of our culture, imagining Him as we want Him to be.

Shoemaker suggests that modern-American Christians have developed a false Christology. This Christology sees Jesus as "divinity devoid of humanity, supremely powerful, wise, righteous, and rich."[8] This false view holds that Jesus was more powerful than any earthly ruler of that time. Adherents to this view admit that He died on a cross, but "the way of the cross was an aberration from His otherwise successful life."[9] They believe that although the cross was necessary for our salvation, it did not define His life. This Christology proclaims that "Jesus came to earth to lift us out of the world's tribulation, and to make us victors in this life."[10] A Jesus like this fits the mold of our success-oriented culture, because He is "always on the side of the powerful."[11]

This false Christology emphasizes health, wealth, and success. It teaches or at least implies that following Jesus will result in prosperity and other forms of human success. Many modern Christians, especially in America, have fallen prey to this understanding of Jesus and the Christian life. A television evangelist epitomized this understanding when he commented on his extravagant lifestyle, "God wants His ministers to go first class."[12]

Shoemaker refers to this kind of belief system as a "false gospel of another Jesus."[13] While such theology might go down well in a society dominated by power and materialism, the Jesus of the Scriptures "does not abolish suffering or rescue us from suffering."[14] Instead, He "teaches us how to bear suffering and sends us into the suffering world with the balms of God."[15]

A search for the historical Jesus must be based on the information we discover about Him in the Bible. We have no other reliable information, and we are not free to create Him in the image of our culture. If we examine Scripture, we will not be able to think of Jesus as a powerful, affluent American. What we find in Scripture stands in stark contrast to the health-and-success pop theology of our time.

We can accurately say that Jesus was a homeless person (see Matt. 8:20). As far as we know, He owned no property, few possessions, and no income of which we have record. By the world's standards He was a failure. Such words may sound shocking to us. We protest that because He is God, He owns the entire universe. Although this is true, such thinking misses the point of His incarnation—God's coming to earth in human flesh. Paul certainly believed and taught that Jesus is the Lord of all creation (see Col. 1:15-17). Yet as He described Jesus' coming in human flesh, he wrote, "For your sakes He became poor so that you through His poverty might become rich" (2 Cor. 8:9). Even the riches promised Jesus' followers through His poverty are not necessarily material riches.

Most persons who loved and followed Jesus were also poor, living on the edges of the social and economic culture. Few of His followers were affluent. Most had no economic, political, or social power. Most were ignored by society—even by the religious power structure. He seemed to gather about Him a society of nobodies.

Why did the Lord of the universe become poor and live among the poor and powerless? The obvious reason is that God wanted to identify Himself with struggling, suffering humanity. Certainly, Jesus could have claimed the world's wealth and power for Himself, but in obedience He laid all of that aside to become a humble servant (see Phil. 2:5-11). While materialistic Americans may not think of Jesus as poor, homeless, and powerless (by the world's standards), this is the accurate biblical picture.

JESUS' MINISTRY: CARING FOR HURTING HUMANITY

Early in His ministry Jesus set the tone for His work on earth. When He was about 30 years old, Jesus presented Himself to John the Baptist for baptism (see Luke 3:21-23). Baptism for Jesus was not only an act of obedience but also a means of identification with the crowds of people John the Baptist had called to repentance. Jesus had no sin of His own; but in baptism, as in His birth and death, He identified Himself with the sinful.

Following His baptism, Jesus experienced temptation in the desert (see Luke 4:1-13). This time of temptation served to clarify and define what kind of Messiah Jesus would be:

• Would He use His divine power to turn stones to bread and thus be a "bread Messiah," using His power to satisfy His own desires and others' material desires?

• Would He throw Himself from the highest point of the temple, testing God and proving to the crowd that He was the Son of God? Surely such a spectacular miracle would win over the people, and they would make Him king.

• Would He worship Satan in order to gain an earthly kingdom?

The answer in each case was a resounding no! Jesus would not be a self-serving, sensational, materialistic ruler.

We are seriously mistaken if we believe this was Jesus' last encounter with Satan. Luke tells us that Satan left Him "until an opportune time" (Luke 4:13). We are not specifically told in the Bible when that time came. However, we are told that He was tempted "in every way, just as we are—yet was without sin" (Heb. 4:15). Whatever specific temptations He faced, we can be sure that Satan tried at every turn of the road to persuade Jesus to use His power in a selfish, spectacular, popular way. Jesus never gave in to these temptations.

Following His temptation in the desert, Jesus apparently began His teaching-and-healing ministry. When He returned to Galilee, He had already made a reputation for Himself: "News about him spread through the whole countryside" (Luke 4:13). He was the topic of conversation when He returned to Nazareth, where He had grown up. When He went into the synagogue, "as was his custom" (Luke 4:16), He was handed a scroll of Isaiah and was asked to read. We can only imagine what the persons in the synagogue were thinking when Jesus stood to read. What would this hometown boy who was becoming a celebrity say?

Jesus took the scroll, unrolled it, and began to read from what we know as Isaiah 61. The gathered worshipers must have listened intently as He read the ancient words:

> "The Spirit of the Sovereign Lord is on me,
>> because he has anointed me
>> to preach good news to the poor.
> He has sent me to proclaim freedom for the prisoners
>> and recovery of sight for the blind,
> to release the oppressed,
>> to proclaim the year of the Lord's favor" (Luke 4:18-19).

When Jesus finished reading, He rolled up the sacred scroll and gave it to the synagogue attendant. Then he sat down because it was customary for rabbis to sit as they talked. Jesus' sermon was brief and to the point. With every eye on Him and every ear listening to Him, Jesus simply said, " 'Today this scripture is fulfilled in your hearing' " (Luke 4:21).

Why did Jesus choose this particular Scripture for what many call His inaugural sermon? The passage is not at all about power. It is about service. The prophet spoke about the Holy Spirit's anointing for preaching good news to the poor, proclaiming freedom for prisoners, giving the blind their sight, and releasing the oppressed. This was hardly what the people expected, and it was nothing like the picture most Jews had of the Messiah. They expected a political, nationalistic, militaristic leader; but Jesus defined Himself as a deliverer of the poor, powerless, and oppressed.

The initial reaction of the people in Nazareth to Jesus' words was positive. They found His words gracious and were especially impressed that such words could come from the lips of "Joseph's son." After all, He was a product of Nazareth. Some of those present in the synagogue had probably known Jesus since He was a young boy. But the positive response was short-lived. Things soon turned ugly in the synagogue: "All the people in the synagogue were furious when they heard this. They got up, drove him out of the town, and took him to the brow of the hill on which the town was built, in order to throw him down the cliff. But he walked right through the crowd and went on his way" (Luke 4:28-30).

Why did the crowd in the synagogue become so angry that they wanted to kill Jesus? The text does not report the details of all that was said and done, but the basic situation is not difficult to reconstruct. Apparently, the crowd asked Jesus to perform a miracle. Perhaps they had heard of His miraculous works elsewhere. Surely, the miracle worker could perform one for the hometown crowd. This must have been the reason for the sharp rebuke Jesus gave to the crowd in the synagogue:

> Jesus said to them, "Surely you will quote this proverb to me: 'Physician, heal yourself! Do here in your hometown what we have heard that you did in Capernaum.'
>
> "I tell you the truth," he continued, "no prophet is accepted in his hometown. I assure you that there were many widows in Israel in Elijah's time, when the sky was shut for three and a half years and there was a severe famine throughout the land. Yet Elijah was not sent to any of them, but to a widow in Zarephath in the region of Sidon. And there were many in Israel with leprosy in the time of Elisha the prophet, yet not one of them was cleansed—only Naaman the Syrian" (Luke 4:23-27).

Jesus refused to demonstrate a miracle for the people. Instead, He reminded them of two great prophets in their history—Elijah and Elisha. These great men did not give a public display of God's power. Significantly, when Elijah ministered to a widow in a time of famine, he chose a woman in Sidon instead of the many needy widows in Israel. When Elisha gave God's healing to a leper, it was given to Naaman, a Syrian, instead of one of the many lepers in Israel. Jesus must have known that reminding these Jews of God's concern for Gentiles would enrage them. Many of them believed that Gentiles were of little value to God unless they became Jewish in their religious practice. To be reminded of God's mercy to Gentiles through the ministry of two of their heroes was more than they were willing to accept. They drove Jesus out and intended to cast Him off the cliff; but Jesus walked right through the crowd, leaving them with their narrow concept of God.

Why did Jesus introduce the issue of God's concern for Gentiles? He wanted the Jewish worshipers not only to know that He had come to minister to the hurting and oppressed but also to understand that this ministry would recognize no barriers of race, culture, or religion.

This incident, recorded in Luke 4, is important because it set the tone for Jesus' ministry over the next three years. Everything He did, everything He taught, every miracle He performed, and even the atoning work He would accomplish on the cross fit perfectly into what He said and did in the synagogue in Nazareth.

While Jesus launched His amazing ministry of service, John the Baptist, who had announced Jesus' coming at the Jordan River, languished in prison because he had spoken out against Herod's sins (see Matt. 14:1-12). John was never released from prison. His life and ministry ended when Herod, following the wishes of the wicked Herodias, had him beheaded. During his imprisonment John apparently began to wonder if Jesus really was the promised Messiah. He sent some of his followers to ask Jesus a very pointed question: " 'Are you the one to come, or should we expect someone else?' " (Matt. 11:3). Many have attempted to explain why John, of all people, would ask this question. After all, was he not the one who had introduced Jesus as the One " 'whose sandals I am not fit to carry' " (Matt. 3:11), the One who " 'will baptize you with the Holy Spirit and with fire' " (Matt. 3:11)? Perhaps, as some have suggested, John's imprisonment, which had ended his powerful ministry, left him so discouraged and demoralized that he experienced doubt. However, I believe there was a deeper reason. We are told that John raised this question when he heard "what Christ was doing" (Matt. 11:2). What was Jesus doing? Even a casual look at the Scriptures reveals that He was teaching, healing, training His disciples, and caring for persons. He was serving, not advancing His own interests or building a power base from which He would assume the expected role of the Messiah. Apparently, even a person as godly as John had difficulty understanding that Jesus came to minister rather than to build an earthly empire.

When Jesus was confronted with John's question, He sent a surprising answer to the baptist: " 'Go back and report to John what you hear and see: The blind receive sight, the lame walk, those who have leprosy are cured, the deaf hear, the dead are raised, and the good news is preached to the poor. Blessed is the man who does not fall away on account of me' " (Matt. 11:4-6). Every proof Jesus offered John spoke of ministry to hurting persons. Like His sermon in Nazareth, this incident clearly presents Jesus as Servant Messiah. He did not come to establish a kingdom that would throw off the cruel shackles of Rome. By the world's standards His would be what one author called "an upside down kingdom."[16] In His kingdom, power would be demonstrated in ministry and service.

An entire study could be made of the ways Jesus expressed His deep caring for spiritual and physical needs. Here we can examine only selected evidences of the ways He cared. Even this brief treatment demonstrates that Jesus had a servant attitude, that He demonstrated this attitude in the way He dealt with persons' needs, and that He taught us to be caring servants.

JESUS' SERVANT ATTITUDE

Although they lived in another time and place, Jesus' disciples were not very different from people today. They wanted to follow Jesus, but they were very interested in what they could gain by doing so. At times they even argued about their individual importance to Jesus' cause. We are told, for example, that "an argument started among the disciples as to which of them would be the greatest" (Luke 9:46). Sometimes the argument escalated into actual jockeying for position. Mark's Gospel records one such incident:

> James and John, the sons of Zebedee, came to him. "Teacher," they said, "we want you to do for us whatever we ask."
> "What do you want me to do for you?" he asked.
> They replied, "Let one of us sit at your right and the other at your left in your glory" (Mark 10:35-37).

Even family members joined the effort to promote their loved ones for positions of power and greatness. Matthew records that James and John's mother interceded on their behalf (see Matt. 20:20-23).

This rivalry for position became a problem for the disciples. After James, John, and their mother requested places of power and prominence for the brothers, the other disciples were angry: "When the ten heard about this, they were indignant with the two brothers" (Matt. 20:24). Jesus reminded them that His kingdom was not one of position and power but of humble service: "Jesus called them together and said, 'You know that the rulers of the Gentiles lord it over them, and their high officials exercise authority over them. Not so with you. Instead, whoever wants to become great among you must be your servant, and whoever wants to be first must be your slave—just as the Son of Man did not come to be served, but to serve, and to give his life as a ransom for many' " (Matt. 20:25-28).

Today people are very competitive. This competition for authority can be seen even in many churches, with Christians vying with one another for recognition and power. The concept of Christian leadership that emerges is very much like that which exists in the non-Christian world. Such an authoritative and assertive concept of leadership can infect the pulpit and the pew. Such a mind-set asks the question, Who's in charge? and seeks to carry on the church's ministry from a position of strength. This type of leadership creates power struggles, producing the same unrest and resentment the disciples experienced. Even worse, such an attitude clouds the real reason God has put us here—to be servants. Tragically, Christians who are overly concerned about their position and power are not likely to spend much effort ministering to hurting persons, who are usually powerless and unable to contribute to their ambitions. Ministry always necessitates a servant attitude.

To help His disciples understand servanthood, Jesus did a beautiful and amazing thing shortly before His death on the cross. The incident is recorded in John's Gospel.

> It was just before the Passover Feast. Jesus knew that the time had come for him to leave this world and go to the Father. Having loved his own who were in the world, he now showed them the full extent of his love.
>
> The evening meal was being served, and the devil had already prompted Judas Iscariot, son of Simon, to betray Jesus. Jesus knew that the Father had put all things under his power, and that he had come from God and was returning to God; so he got up from the meal, took off his outer clothing, and wrapped a towel around his waist. After that, he poured water into a basin and began to wash his disciples' feet, drying them with the towel that was wrapped around him.
>
> When he had finished washing their feet, he put on his clothes and returned to his place. "Do you understand what I have done for you?" he asked them. "You call me 'Teacher' and 'Lord,' and rightly so, for that is what I am. Now that I, your Lord and Teacher, have washed your feet, you also should wash one another's feet. I have set you an example that you should do as I have done for you. I tell you the truth, no servant is greater than his master, nor is a messenger greater than the one who sent him. Now that you know these things, you will be blessed if you do them" (John 13:1-5,12-17).

Foot washing was a social necessity in that time. People traveled dusty roads with sandals on their feet. Cleanliness and comfort dictated that provision be made for washing feet. A host usually provided water for a guest to wash his own feet. Sometimes a slave washed others' feet, although a Hebrew slave could not be compelled to perform this lowly task. Sometimes, as a sign of exceptional love, a disciple might wash his master's feet.

Try to imagine the shock and disbelief that night when Jesus filled a basin with water, wrapped a towel around His waist, and began to wash each disciple's feet. The disciples must have watched in stunned silence as their Master did what even a slave would hesitate to do.

Jesus explained His reason for washing the disciples' feet. He was and is Lord. Yet He had taken the attitude of a lowly slave. The obvious lesson was that they must be willing to serve one another, even in the most menial ways. Such an attitude is an inversion of the world's way of doing things. This beautiful account teaches that service and ministry are the measures of true greatness. This attitude always undergirds ministry. Unless we see ourselves as servants, we are not likely to pay the price that ministry requires.

JESUS' SERVANT TEACHING

Jesus taught us how to serve, minister, and relate to persons. In Matthew 5:43-47 He told us how we are to relate to our enemies. In Matthew 6:1-4 He showed us how we should give to the needy. Matthew 5:1-12 names the attitudes that are to characterize our lives.

The supreme example of ministry in Jesus' teaching is found in Luke 10. A teacher of the law challenged Jesus by asking the question " 'What must I do to inherit eternal life?' " (v. 25). Jesus answered the challenge by issuing one of His own: " 'What is written in the law? ... How do you read it?' " (v. 26). The expert in the law combined Scripture from the Shema (Deut. 6:3; 11:13) and Leviticus 19:18 in his answer: " ' "Love the Lord your God with all your heart and with all your soul and with all your strength and with all your mind"; and, "Love your neighbor as yourself" ' " (v. 27). Jesus commended the teacher's answer (see v. 28), but the man was not finished. He had another question: " 'Who is my neighbor?' " (v. 29). In response to this question, Jesus told one of the most remarkable stories in history, the parable of the good Samaritan. This parable has become so much a part of our culture that almost everyone knows that a "good Samaritan" is someone who helps another person.

A man who was traveling from Jerusalem to Jericho was robbed, beaten, and left beside the road. A priest came by, saw him, but did not help. A Levite came by, saw him, made a wide path around him, and went on. Finally, a Samaritan passed by. He too saw the beaten man but stopped, rendered first aid, took the man on his own donkey to a place where the man could be cared for, and paid for his care (see Luke 10:30-35).

Now it was Jesus' turn to ask a question: " 'Which of these three do you think was a neighbor to the man who fell into the hands of robbers?' " (v. 36). The answer was too obvious to miss: " 'The one who had mercy on him' " (v. 37). Then Jesus ended the encounter by saying, " 'Go and do likewise' " (v. 37).

Jesus' story is filled with meaning. The parable was a pointed indictment of the kind of religion that does not care about the needs of a broken person. The priest and the Levite were religious professionals, but they did not have time or concern to care for a beaten man. Perhaps they feared for their own safety or simply had too many "religious" things to do.

True neighborliness and true religion notice a beaten person. The Samaritan not only *looked* at the man by the road but also *saw* him. He took time to care and minister. No doubt he got his hands dirty and bloody. He took time he could have used for his own purposes. He paid a price, for ministry is always costly.

The parable was made more poignant because its hero was a Samaritan. The Jews of that day considered the Samaritans to be outcasts, but this man understood something the religious leaders had forgotten: persons are important and are worth making the effort to redeem and help.

Perhaps no part of Jesus' teaching is more appropriate to our time than the parable of the good Samaritan. We live in a dangerous and broken world, where many have been beaten and left to die alone. The abuse of children, spouses, and the elderly is daily news. Sadly, this abuse is often committed by family members. Many in our society are victimized by seemingly uncontrollable crime and violence. Alcohol and other drugs leave the lives of millions in shambles. The homeless fill our streets. The horror of AIDS threatens the whole population. Sin brings misery, pain, and death. If we want to know who our neighbor is, we need to understand that this hurting, broken world is our needy neighborhood.

Too often, the church is regarded as an escape from the hurting world. Christians go about their business in a way similar to the priest's and the Levite's actions toward the beaten man—as if the pain were not there. The Samaritan is a picture of one who has God's heart for hurting persons. The world cries for good-Samaritan Christians, who take time to notice and who pay the price to care.

This parable, like many of Jesus' teachings, points to the supreme truth that service and ministry to others are the ways we truly demonstrate love for God.

JESUS' SERVANT ACTIONS

Jesus' servant dedication was obvious not only in His attitude and teaching but especially in His actions toward hurting persons. His miracles of forgiveness and healing fill the pages of the four Gospels. A summary statement of this ministry is found in Matthew 9: "Jesus went through all the towns and villages, teaching in their synagogues, preaching the good news of the kingdom and healing every disease and sickness. When he saw the crowds, he had compassion on them, because they were harassed and helpless, like sheep without a shepherd" (vv. 35-36).

Jesus saw the people as "harassed and helpless." Literally, they were distressed and prostrate. A. T. Robertson suggests that they were cast down to the ground, as if drunk or mortally wounded.[17] Furthermore, they were like sheep without a shepherd, an image that speaks of helplessness and a lack of direction. When Jesus saw these people, He "had compassion on them." The Greek word used here is a form of the word *splagchnon*, which in its various forms speaks of sympathy that comes from inside, far more than a surface or passing sympathy. It is a sympathy that feels for the other person. Jesus felt deeply about these distressed people. To express this concern, He preached the good news to them and healed their sicknesses and diseases. He put His love into action by ministering to their spiritual and physical needs. This pattern was consistent throughout Jesus' life and ministry. He saw persons in their sin and hurts. He cared about what was happening to them, and His care went to the depths of His being. He met human needs, both spiritual and physical.

Many examples of Jesus' compassion toward persons in need could be given. One is especially poignant and descriptive:

> A man with leprosy came to him and begged him on his knees, "If you are willing, you can make me clean."
>
> Filled with compassion, Jesus reached out his hand and touched the man. "I am willing," he said. "Be clean!" Immediately the leprosy left him and he was cured.
>
> Jesus sent him away at once with a strong warning: "See that you don't tell this to anyone. But go, show yourself to the priest and offer the sacrifices that Moses commanded for your cleansing, as a testimony to them." Instead he went out and began to talk freely, spreading the news. As a result, Jesus could no longer enter a town openly but stayed outside in lonely places. Yet the people still came to him from everywhere (Mark 1:40-45).

Leprosy was the most dreaded disease of the first century. It had both physical and social implications: physical because of the devastating effect it had on the body, social because the person with leprosy was excluded from family, work, friends, and places of worship. A leper was actually required to wear torn clothes; let his hair hang loose; and cry, "Unclean!" if anyone came too near.

The leper who approached Jesus was pitiful. He fell on his knees and begged for Jesus' help. Notice his words: " 'If you are willing, you can make me clean' " (v. 40). He seemed to have no doubt that Jesus could help him. Rather, he wondered whether Jesus would. Undoubtedly, his dreaded disease had shattered any sense of self-worth he ever had. How could he believe that Jesus would be willing to help him? After all, everyone else had shut him out.

Once again we are told that Jesus was "filled with compassion" toward him (v. 41). Then Jesus did the unthinkable—He touched the man. Touching a leper was not only unsafe but also illegal. Henry E. Turlington writes, "By this little act Jesus identified himself with the leper; it made him a partner in the man's ritual defilement."[18] Certainly, Jesus did not have to touch the man. He could have stood the required distance from him to speak the healing word, but He touched him. Very likely, it was the first touch the man had felt in a long time. To others he was an unclean leper, but to Jesus he was a man—a man worth touching and healing.

This story typifies Jesus' three-year ministry. He found persons where they were, loved them unconditionally, and reached out to minister to them. His ultimate expression of this great love was giving His life on the cross for all people.

MINISTRY AND THE FINAL JUDGMENT

Matthew 24–25 has eschatological themes; that is, it deals with events that will take place at Jesus' second coming and the end of the world (see Matt. 24:3). One of the most powerful images of that time is the picture of the judgment found in Matthew 25:31-46:

> "When the Son of Man comes in his glory, and all the angels with him, he will sit on his throne in heavenly glory. All the nations will be gathered before him, and he will separate the people one from another as a shepherd separates the sheep from the goats. He will put the sheep on his right and the goats on his left.
>
> "Then the King will say to those on his right, 'Come, you

who are blessed by my Father; take your inheritance, the kingdom prepared for you since the creation of the world. For I was hungry and you gave me something to eat, I was thirsty and you gave me something to drink, I was a stranger and you invited me in, I needed clothes and you clothed me, I was sick and you looked after me, I was in prison and you came to visit me.'

"Then the righteous will answer him, 'Lord, when did we see you hungry and feed you, or thirsty and give you something to drink? When did we see you a stranger and invite you in, or needing clothes and clothe you? When did we see you sick or in prison and go to visit you?'

"The King will reply, 'I tell you the truth, whatever you did for one of the least of these brothers of mine, you did for me.'

"Then he will say to those on his left, 'Depart from me, you who are cursed, into the eternal fire prepared for the devil and his angels. For I was hungry and you gave me nothing to eat, I was thirsty and you gave me nothing to drink, I was a stranger and you did not invite me in, I needed clothes and you did not clothe me, I was sick and in prison and you did not look after me.'

"They also will answer, 'Lord, when did we see you hungry or thirsty or a stranger or needing clothes or sick or in prison, and did not help you?'

"He will reply, 'I tell you the truth, whatever you did not do for one of the least of these, you did not do for me.'

"Then they will go away to eternal punishment, but the righteous to eternal life" (Matt. 25:31-46).

Some interpreters suggest that this passage refers to the judgment of the nations rather than to the judgment of individuals (see v. 32). According to this view, the nations of the world will be judged for their treatment of the Jews, Jesus' "brothers" (v. 40). Even if you agree with this view of end times, you make a tragic mistake if you do not apply these powerful words to individual action or inaction toward the needy in every period of history.

Scripture can best speak to us if we do not try to fit it into a predetermined system or interpretation. Taking this passage at face value, we recognize that Jesus taught that feeding the hungry, giving drink to the thirsty, welcoming the stranger, clothing the ragged, caring for the sick, and visiting the prisoner are like doing those things for Jesus. On the other hand, closing our hearts and hands to persons with these needs is like turning away and refusing to help Jesus.

Jesus called these hurting and needy ones " 'these brothers of mine' " (v. 40). This should not surprise us. Everything Jesus did—His birth, His miracles, His teaching, His death—makes clear that He is a brother to the weak and fallen. We dare not turn away from His needy brothers and sisters.

A young woman was on her way to work one evening when she saw a beaten woman staggering along the street. The woman was bleeding; and all of her clothing, except for her underclothes, had been ripped off by her drunken, enraged boyfriend. The young woman stopped, covered the woman with some of her own clothes, comforted her, and took her to a shelter where she could be safe. At a recent prayer vigil for victims of abuse, that brave young woman received a commendation for the help she gave to the frightened, hurting woman.

All of us admire someone who cares enough to help someone in need, but admiration is not enough. We must ask ourselves, *What am I doing to reach out in love to hurting persons?*

The Bible clearly reveals God as a Father who cares for all of His children, especially those who are hurting or in need. The teachings of Scripture in both the Old Testament and the New Testament are the foundation on which ministry evangelism is built. Most importantly, Jesus' life, teaching, miracles, and death reveal that He came to minister and to give His life for others. If we follow Him, then we must follow His example.

Charles Roesel, the pastor of First Baptist Church, Leesburg, Florida, likes to paraphrase his favorite Scripture passage, Matthew 25:39-40: " 'When did we see You hungry, naked, homeless, or hurting?' Then the pastor will smile as he gives Jesus' response: 'When you ministered to the least of these my brothers, you ministered to Me.' "

---

[1]Roy L. Honeycutt, Jr., "Deuteronomy" in *The Broadman Bible Commentary*, vol. 2 (Nashville: Broadman Press, 1970), 233.
[2]Ronald E. Clements, "Leviticus" in *The Broadman Bible Commentary*, vol. 2 (Nashville: Broadman Press, 1970), 51–52.
[3]Robert N. Sanders, *Radical Voices in the Wilderness, The Social Implications of the Prophets* (Waco: Word, 1970), 20.
[4]Kyle M. Yates, *Preaching from the Prophets* (Nashville: Broadman Press, 1942), 32–33.
[5]Sanders, *Radical Voices in the Wilderness*, 30.
[6]Ibid., 32.
[7]H. Stephen Shoemaker, *Strength in Weakness* (Nashville: Broadman Press, 1989), 148.
[8]Ibid., 149.

[9]Ibid.
[10]Ibid.
[11]Ibid.
[12]Ibid., 153.
[13]Ibid., 148.
[14]Ibid., 151.
[15]Ibid.
[16]Gayle D. Erwin, *The Jesus Style* (Waco: Word, 1983), 4.
[17]Archibald Thomas Robertson, *The Gospel According to Matthew*, vol. 1 in *Word Pictures in the New Testament* (Nashville: Broadman Press, 1930), 76.
[18]Henry E. Turlington, "Mark" in *The Broadman Bible Commentary*, vol. 8 (Nashville: Broadman Press, 1969), 277.

3

His Body in His World

JOAN AND DAVE MCCULLEN assumed leadership of the Rescue Mission of First Baptist Church, Leesburg, Florida, in 1988. Since that time they have ministered to more than 1,500 men who came from the ragged edges of life. Many of the men were addicted to alcohol and other drugs, and some were fleeing from the law. All came to Leesburg with broken hearts and shattered lives. Many of the men have trusted in Jesus Christ as Savior, and their lives have turned around. Some have found work in Leesburg and worship regularly with the congregation of First Baptist Church.

Joan McCullen wrote of her spiritual pilgrimage and call to service:

One Sunday morning in the summer of 1969 I responded to the altar call and gave my heart to the Lord Jesus Christ. Even though I had made a commitment to Christ as a teenager, I constantly vacillated between the world's way and Jesus' way, never making a total commitment. How I praise Him for the peace that passes understanding and for the work He began that day in 1969.

My husband and I were directed into a small Southern Baptist church that would soon change the course of our lives. There the Lord taught us to reach out to the unlovely, the wayward, and the poor, fulfilling Matthew 25:35-36.

In 1984 we became members of First Baptist Church in Leesburg. When we served as the temporary directors of the Rescue Mission in the summer of 1987, our hearts were bonded with love to this ministry. When our pastor, Charles Roesel, asked us to become the full-time directors of this ministry, the decision was easy. The Lord had already led our hearts in this direction.

I never cease to be awed by the way the Lord had prepared us through the years, pruning, polishing, and teaching us. I thank

God that He has provided grace sufficient for all my sin and for the sins of all who call out to Him. Praise be to God for the great works He is doing!

Leesburg's First Baptist Church is dynamic, alive, and involved in ministry to hurting persons. The members of this church take seriously Paul's words to the Corinthian church: "You show that you are a letter from Christ, the result of our ministry, written not with ink but with the Spirit of the living God, not on tablets of stone, but on tablets of human hearts" (2 Cor. 3:3). By recognizing and meeting human needs, the ministries of this church are like a love letter from God to hurting persons. More importantly, the ministries of First Baptist always seek to share Jesus Christ, who alone can meet all persons' deepest needs.

Although God often works through many channels to meet human needs—individuals, families, social agencies, Christian organizations, and government—the primary agent for His activity is the church. Early in His ministry Jesus responded to Simon's confession " 'You are the Christ, the Son of the living God' " by saying, " 'On this rock I will build my church' " (Matt. 16:16-18). Jesus is the founder and owner of the church. It belongs to Him and exists to serve His purposes in the world.

Iranaeus, a leading second-century Christian, wrote: "Where the church is, there is the Spirit of God; and where the Spirit of God is, there is the church, and every kind of grace."[1] Ministry evangelism is a vital function of the church of the Lord Jesus Christ. In this chapter we will examine the church's meaning, purpose, and calling. This study will be essential if we are to understand what it means to be God's people and to join His redemptive, healing work in this world.

THE CHURCH'S MINISTRY IN NEW TESTAMENT TIMES

After Jesus died and rose from the grave, He spent time instructing His little group of believers. No doubt when He died, they gave up all hope of carrying out all He had taught them; but His resurrection changed everything. He was alive! The question was no longer how they would go on without Him. The question was and still is, How are His followers to carry out His mission?

The Book of Acts provides an exciting record of what followed. Luke wrote: "After his suffering, he showed himself to these men and gave many convincing proofs that he was alive. He appeared to them over a period of forty days and spoke about the kingdom of God" (Acts 1:3). We do not know all Jesus said to His followers during this period, but we have some specifics. We know, for example, that He commanded them to wait in Jerusalem for the gift of the Holy Spirit (see Acts 1:4-5). We also know that He gave them a tremendously large assignment: " 'You will receive power when the Holy Spirit comes on you, and you will be my witnesses in Jerusalem, and in all Judea, and Samaria, and to the ends of the earth' " (Acts 1:8). Their assigned territory was the whole world! Jesus' message was to be given to all, and this group of believers was responsible for delivering it. Jesus' command is even more startling when we realize that it was addressed to about 120 persons (see Acts 1:15).

The words of this challenging commission are Jesus' last recorded words on this earth. Luke records: "After he said this, he was taken up before their very eyes, and a cloud hid him from their sight" (Acts 1:9). The startled disciples watched as He disappeared from view. No doubt His final words still rang in their ears: " 'You will be my witnesses.' " These believers were faced with a task so far-reaching that they could not have understood all of its implications and demands. That task was world evangelization. Our generation of Christians is still working at it.

Jesus' followers must have understood the urgency of their Lord's final command, for they wasted no time getting started. Leaving the Mount of Olives, where Jesus had ascended before their eyes, they returned to Jerusalem to an upstairs room and began a time of earnest prayer (see Acts 1:14). Apparently, they felt the need to be at their full leadership strength, because they quickly replaced the traitor Judas, choosing Matthias to take his place in the twelve. The believers waited and prayed for the promised power. They did not have to wait long. God answered their prayers in ways far beyond their imagining: "When the day of Pentecost came, they were all together in one place. Suddenly a sound like the blowing of a violent wind came from heaven and filled the whole house where they were sitting. They saw what seemed to be tongues of fire that separated and came to rest on each of them. All of them were filled with the Holy Spirit and began to speak in other tongues as the Spirit enabled them" (Acts 2:1-4).

We can only partially understand what happened to those believers that day. They heard a sound like a mighty wind and saw something that looked like tongues of fire. We can only imagine what happened, but the important point is that the believers were completely and forever changed. Jesus' promise that they would receive power became a reality. They were filled with the Holy Spirit.

We do not have to wonder how these believers used this tremendous power. They began to fulfill their assignment of witnessing to the whole world on the day of Pentecost. Jews "from every nation under heaven"

(Acts 2:5) were in Jerusalem for the celebration of Pentecost. Although all of them were Jews or proselytes, they spoke many different languages. The believers began to speak with other tongues; that is, God enabled them to speak in many languages. They used this miracle of speaking and hearing to witness. The people of many different nations were amazed that these followers of Jesus were " 'declaring the wonders of God in our own tongues' " (Acts 2:11).

Peter took advantage of the stir caused by his fellow disciples' witnessing. Raising his voice for attention, he preached the masterful sermon of Pentecost, clearly witnessing to Jesus, who was crucified and resurrected (see Acts 2:14-36). The Holy Spirit's power was so real that people were brought under great conviction: "When the people heard this, they were cut to the heart and said to Peter and the other apostles, 'Brothers, what shall we do?' " (Acts 2:37).

Peter responded to their cries: " 'Repent and be baptized, every one of you, in the name of Jesus Christ for the forgiveness of your sins. And you will receive the gift of the Holy Spirit. The promise is for you and your children and for all who are far off—for all whom the Lord our God will call' " (Acts 2:38-39).

The response was amazing. On that one day about three thousand people believed, were baptized, and were added to the church. The task of evangelizing the world had begun.

The church's evangelistic thrust did not stop with the amazing events of Pentecost. This was only the beginning. Amid the teaching, fellowshipping, worshiping, rejoicing, and sharing, outreach to the lost continued: "The Lord added to their number daily those who were being saved" (Acts 2:47).

Significantly, in the early church, ministry was coupled with evangelism from the beginning. Following the tremendous ingathering of Pentecost, the body of believers began to share with those in need. Many even sold everything they had and gave "to anyone as he had need" (Acts 2:45). Although the context leads us to believe that much of this sharing was with needy believers, the principle emerges that sharing the gospel goes hand in hand with reaching out to hurting, needy persons.

Even if the earliest ministry was to fellow believers, it was not long before the circle of ministry widened. Peter and John were on their way into the temple for prayer. Sitting at the temple gate was a beggar whose physical disabilities had reduced him to poverty and dependence. The destitute man probably felt that the house dedicated to God's worship was the best place to ask for help. When he saw Peter and John, he asked them for money. Luke records that "Peter looked straight at him, as did John" (Acts 3:4). Why does Scripture make the point that they looked at him? Probably because others passed by without noticing the man at all, and even some who dropped a few coins as they passed might have done so from habit without really noticing the man. In contrast, these two men of God cared enough to look at him. Naturally, the man expected that they would give him money and was probably disappointed when Peter said, " 'Silver or gold I do not have' " (Acts 3:6). Imagine how his disappointment was turned to surprise and joy when Peter continued: " 'But what I have I give you. In the name of Jesus Christ of Nazareth, walk' " (Acts 3:6). Then Peter took him by the hand and helped him stand on his feet. Soon the man was walking, jumping, and praising God as a crowd watched in amazement (see Acts 3:7-10).

What happened next is a wonderful example of the way evangelism and ministry were linked in the early church. Peter used the excitement created by the man's healing to tell the crowd about Jesus (see Acts 3:11-26). Peter and John had reached out to a man who desperately needed ministry. As a result, they reached into the man's heart, as well as the hearts of many in the crowd, with the saving message of Jesus Christ.

Rapid growth continued in the Jerusalem church. Soon the number of believers had grown to about five thousand (see Acts 4:4). The Jewish religious establishment tried to slow the growth by calling Peter and John to account for what was happening. Even before the powerful religious council Peter proclaimed, " 'Salvation is found in no one else, for there is no other name under heaven given to men by which we must be saved' " (Acts 4:12). When the perplexed religious leaders warned Peter and John not to preach about Jesus anymore, they responded, " 'We cannot help speaking about what we have seen and heard' " (Acts 4:20).

The threats of the religious authorities drove the believers to their knees. They did not pray to be spared suffering. Rather, they prayed: " 'Now, Lord, consider their threats and enable your servants to speak your word with great boldness. Stretch out your hand to heal and perform miraculous signs and wonders through the name of your holy servant Jesus' " (Acts 4:29-30). They asked not for personal deliverance from danger but for boldness to speak His word and for miracles of healing to glorify Jesus and meet human needs.

The believers simultaneously witnessed to the power of Jesus' resurrection and met needs generously. So loving and caring was their fellowship that "there were no needy persons among them" (Acts 4:34). Many believers even sold their houses and land and brought the proceeds to the apostles. Then the money was "distributed to anyone as he had need" (Acts 4:35). For these early believers, preaching the good news about Jesus and ministering to persons' needs were complementary tasks.

The threat of persecution hung like a dark cloud over the earliest church in Jerusalem. When it finally hit with full fury, most believers were forced to flee (see Acts 8:1). However, this time of great suffering fanned the flames of evangelistic outreach as "those who had been scattered preached the word wherever they went" (Acts 8:4). The good news of Jesus spread with explosive force into Judea, Samaria, and beyond. The message that was initially preached mainly to Jews made its way to the Gentile world (see Acts 8:26-40; 10).

The conversion of Saul of Tarsus (see Acts 9) is a pivotal event in history. When this brilliant, zealous, tireless enemy of Jesus and His people became a believer, the floodgates of worldwide evangelism opened. This remarkable man, known to us as the apostle Paul, made clear by his words and actions that the gospel of Christ was a message for all people. Using the church at Antioch as a base, Paul and other spiritual giants like Barnabas, Silas, and Timothy visited the great Gentile cities of the Roman Empire. In these great cultural and trade centers of the world these missionaries preached Christ and founded churches. What started as a spark in Jerusalem began to break into flames all over the Roman world.

This exciting history of the spread of the gospel fills the remaining pages of the Book of Acts. This portion of God's Word gives much more attention to the spread of the gospel than to ministry to hurting persons. However, the emphasis on caring was never lost. Acts records numerous healings as the apostles concerned themselves with physical needs as well as spiritual needs. For example, Paul and Silas took time to deliver a slave girl in Philippi from demonic powers that kept her from living a normal life (see Acts 16:16-39). Even when Paul was shipwrecked en route to Rome, where he would stand trial, he healed the sick father of Publius, an official on the island of Malta. When word of this healing spread, "the rest of the sick on the island came and were cured" (Acts 28:9). Winning persons to faith in Jesus was the priority, but concern for physical needs was never absent.

As the early church changed from mostly Jewish in membership to predominantly Gentile, conflict arose over the very nature of the Christian message. The question was, Could Gentiles become followers of Jesus without first adopting some of Judaism's legalistic requirements? Paul and his associates proclaimed a gospel of grace apart from legalism. Gentiles were responding in great numbers to this message, and some leaders in

Jerusalem had difficulty accepting these converts. Some leaders even insisted that the Gentile believers be circumcised and submit to various Jewish practices (see Acts 15:1-2). Paul and Barnabas, along with other believers in Antioch, were commissioned by the Antioch church to go to Jerusalem to meet with the apostles about this matter. Bible students identify the meeting in Jerusalem, described in Acts 15, as one of the most important ever held.

Although Judaizing, the idea that persons must follow Jewish customs to be Christians, would continue to plague the church for years (Paul dealt with it in most of his letters to the churches), the Jerusalem Council defined the nature of the gospel. Had Paul and his friends lost that battle, all Christian history would be markedly different. When Paul wrote his letter to the Galatians, he reflected on the decisions made at that crucial Jerusalem Council. He wrote of the affirmation given to the gospel by Peter, James, and John when they gave Paul and Barnabas "the right hand of fellowship" (Gal. 2:9). Reflecting further on that historic meeting, Paul wrote: "All they asked was that we should continue to remember the poor, the very thing I was eager to do" (Gal. 2:10). Even in the midst of the most important theological summit of Christian history, both sides expressed concern for the poor. As always, the proclamation of the message of salvation and Christian social concern marched hand in hand.

The congregation of First Baptist Church in Leesburg, Florida, is often reminded that the church exists for evangelism as a fire exists for burning. This conviction directs every ministry the church performs. Church members have learned that social ministry alone is not the church's work. On the other hand, they have discovered that meeting persons' needs is an effective way to share the gospel. God's people do not have to choose between ministering to hurting persons and winning persons to Jesus Christ. Like the believers in the earliest church, Christians today will find that caring for persons in need often opens the door of opportunity for introducing them to Jesus, the ultimate answer to every need in life.

Kelly, a 16-year-old, came to the Pregnancy-Care Center for a free pregnancy test. Kelly was confused, afraid, and worried about her mother's reaction if the test proved positive. Before administering the test, the center's director asked Kelly what she intended to do if she was pregnant. "I don't believe in abortion," she replied, "but I really don't have any other choice." Her boyfriend had already expressed his preference—abortion.

The test confirmed Kelly's suspicion that she was pregnant. Tears came to her eyes when she heard the news. Because the Pregnancy-Care Center helps women who are faced with unwanted pregnancy explore alternatives to abortion, Kelly was shown a video, given literature, and counseled about the decision she would have to make about her unborn baby. She left that day with a lot to think about. She knew her boyfriend and her mother would insist that she get an abortion, but she wanted to read the literature and educate herself about abortion and the alternatives before she made her decision. The director of the Pregnancy-Care Center pledged her love and prayers to Kelly and told her that the center's staff would always be available to her, no matter what she decided.

A few weeks later, Kelly returned with good news. Even though she faced intense pressure from her mother and her boyfriend, she had decided to have her baby. The staff at the Pregnancy-Care Center worked with Kelly to support her courageous decision. Arrangements were made for clothing, prenatal care, and other medical assistance. When Kelly came to receive her clothing, the director shared the gospel with her. Kelly received Jesus as her personal Savior and Lord. Her child would have a Christian mother.

When Kelly called to announce the birth of her daughter, Heather Lynn, she was happy and excited. Her family was also excited—including her mother. When Kelly's mother saw her precious granddaughter, she exclaimed, "Oh, Kelly, I'm so glad you didn't have an abortion!"

Kelly married the baby's father. Unfortunately, the marriage ended in divorce; but Kelly has continued to grow as a person and as a Christian. Heather Lynn, whose life was almost ended by abortion, is growing and learning every day.

Kelly's story is an example of caring love in action, of redemptive love that does not give up on persons. The Pregnancy-Care Center's director wrote: "When women like Kelly come to the Pregnancy-Care Center, most of them come because of the effects of sin in their lives, and it might be easy to look down on them in judgment. But that attitude is not Christlike. Instead, we bend over to help them up—and to help them find new life in Christ."

THE NATURE OF THE CHURCH: NEW TESTAMENT IMAGES

Because a church's purpose is to carry on Christ's work of meeting persons' physical and spiritual needs, we need to have an accurate picture of what a church should be. What is a church? Different answers are given to this question:

- A building or a complex of buildings in which religious activities are held
- An organization with specific interests and purposes, much like a club or a civic organization

- The repository of ancient religious and moral truth
- An essential cultural entity—the place for baptisms, weddings, funerals, and other important events
- A force for social and political change—civil rights or prolife causes, for example

A measure of truth may be found in all of these understandings of the church. Churches are often identified by their buildings. They are places where significant life events take place. Churches teach specific doctrinal and moral truths. Churches are often forces for social change. They are places we go and to which we belong. They are a vital part of a community's cultural life. But while all of these understandings have validity, they fall far short of the biblical teaching.

In seeking to understand what the church is, we must ask this related question: Whose church is it? Does the church belong to the community in which it exists? Does it belong to its members? Does the church belong to the leaders or ecclesiastical powers? Does the church belong to an influential power group? Who owns the church?

In *The Doctrine of the Priesthood of Believers* Walter Shurden tells of a man who commented that the letters *FBC* did not mean *First Baptist Church* when applied to his church. Rather, he said, *FBC* stood for *Fred's Baptist Church*.[2] Apparently, some members of that congregation felt that Fred was in charge of the church. Unfortunately, too often we do not understand who really owns the church, who is really in charge of its worship and work.

The question of who owns the church is easy to answer from a biblical standpoint. One day at Caesarea Philippi Jesus asked His disciples an important question: " 'Who do people say the Son of Man is?' " (Matt. 16:13). The disciples responded by repeating the many ideas that were circulating about Jesus. Then Jesus asked them an even more important question: " 'Who do you say I am?' " (Matt. 16:15). Simon Peter, speaking for the group, said, " 'You are the Christ, the Son of the living God' " (Matt. 16:16). Jesus responded that the truth Peter had spoken was not from humans but by revelation from God. Then He said, " 'On this rock I will build my church, and the gates of Hades will not overcome it' " (Matt. 16:18).

The church belongs to Jesus Christ. Although individual members of a congregation might contribute to a church's work and might participate in decisions about the church's ministries, the church does not belong to the members of the congregation. Even though dedicated pastors, staff ministers, and lay leaders give direction and leadership to the church, the church does not belong to its leaders. The church—every church—belongs to Jesus

Christ. Remember what He said to His disciples: " 'I will build *my* church' " (Matt. 16:18, emphasis added).

Scripture also answers the question of what the church is supposed to be. According to Paul Minear in *Images of the Church in the New Testament,* between 80 and 100 different pictures of the church are included in the New Testament.[3] Some of these images are descriptive but are used sparingly. However, several powerful images of the church in the New Testament help us understand the church's nature and responsibility. These biblical truths are important if we are to understand the concept of winning persons to faith in Christ by caring for them in daily, practical ways.

The ekklesia *of God. Church* is the English translation of the Greek word *ekklesia.* This word was used to report Jesus' words at Caesarea Philippi: " 'I will build my church' " (Matt.16:18). *Ekklesia* is used in the New Testament 112 times to designate the church.[4] The term is also used more than 100 times in the Septuagint, the Greek translation of the Old Testament that was commonly used in Jesus' time. In the Greek translation of the Old Testament *ekklesia* is used to translate the Hebrew word *gahal,* which means *assembly.* Although this word was used in a variety of ways, it was used in the Old Testament to refer to God's people. *Ekklesia* carries the meaning of *the called out.* The early Christians "perceived themselves as called out by God in Jesus Christ for a special purpose and that their status was a privileged one in Jesus Christ."[5] The church, then, is the *ekklesia* of God, His called-out people.

The most frequent use of *ekklesia* in the New Testament is to identify a congregation of believers in a certain location, such as "the church of God in Corinth" (1 Cor. 1:2). But the word also refers to the entire called-out people of God. Thus, the word has both local and universal applications. Bill J. Leonard reminds us, "The New Testament *ekklesia* was a visible community of believers which exercised significant local distinctiveness, even autonomy, but was in no way spiritually independent of other Christian congregations."[6]

If the church is God's people who have been called out, it is important to determine from what and to what the church has been called. Clearly, the church is made up of people God has called out of the world and has set apart to Himself as His very own. Just as clearly, God has called His people to something: to do His work in the world. Jesus prayed for His followers, " 'My prayer is not that you take them out of the world but that you protect them from the evil one' " (John 17:15). Jesus never intended that His people—His church—exist as a safe island, remote from the world's hurt and brokenness. Rather, His purpose was that His called-out people recognize that they are called to the tasks of ministry and witness in a world of sin.

Sometimes we are more concerned with preserving the traditions of the church as we know it than with doing Christ's work in the world as He commands it. Bill Hull observes: "The average evangelical church in North America exists for itself. Churches are preoccupied with themselves, their routines, locations, facilities, and filling up their buildings for performances."[7] As proof of his point, Hull refers to a survey by Bob Gilliam indicating that in today's church it takes 100 adults an entire year to win 1.7 persons to Christ. Reflecting on this tragic statistic, Hull writes: "Most churches could do a better job of reaching those in need of Christ if they would close down the church and hire one person to go door-to-door. In ten hours a week, such a person could reap a greater harvest than do many of our churches."[8]

When God called His people *out* of the world, He called them *to* a mission. That mission is to be His people *in* the world. This always involves caring and witness. God's purpose is redemptive. He is concerned about persons—including hurting, needy persons. The church is called out to carry on His work.

Koinonia *of the Spirit.* "If *ekklesia* describes the community of the church, *koinonia* describes the nature of that community."[9] *Koinonia*—fellowship—is a recurring theme in the New Testament, especially in Paul's writings. Paul refers to the *koinonia* of the Holy Spirit (see 2 Cor. 13:14; Phil. 2:1). He affirmed that believers have *koinonia* with the Father and the Son (see 1 Cor. 1:9). First Corinthians 10:16-17 relates the idea of *koinonia* to the sharing of the bread and the cup. Acts 2:42 presents *koinonia* as one element that characterized the church after Pentecost:[10] "They devoted themselves to the apostles' teaching and to the fellowship, to the breaking of bread and to prayer."

We use the English word *fellowship* to translate *koinonia.* Actually, this is a weak word to explain the true meaning of *koinonia. Koinonia* is more than a picture of congenial, like-minded persons who enjoy one another's company and do things together. *Koinonia* means "to share in, to have communion with, to be involved in partnership together. It involves a dual partnership that involves God, ourselves, and others."[11]

The use of *koinonia* to describe a deep level of communion is seen in 1 Corinthians 10:16, in which Paul addressed the nature of the Lord's Supper. Paul wrote: "Is not the cup of thanksgiving for which we give thanks a participation in the blood of Christ? And is not the bread that we break a participation in the body of Christ?" The word *participation* in that verse is the *New International Version*'s translation of *koinonia*. The *King James Version* translates the word as *communion*. The idea is sharing in Jesus' sacrifice by observing the Lord's Supper. Really, it is more than sharing; it is participating in Christ's suffering through the memorial feast.

When Paul commended the churches of Macedonia for generously giving to meet other Christians' needs, he wrote: "They urgently pleaded with us for the privilege of sharing in this service to the saints" (2 Cor. 8:4). The word *sharing* is the *New International Version*'s translation of the Greek word *koinonian*. The *King James Version* translates the word as *fellowship* in 2 Corinthians 8:4. Again, the idea is sharing at a deep level. In this case it speaks of sharing with fellow believers, giving of themselves and their means to those who were in need.

As the *koinonia* of the Spirit, the church is a community of sharing and support. This fellowship is not surface goodwill but involvement with others at the deepest level of compassion. Of course, this applies to relationships among believers, but by implication it also applies to sharing life with the world in Christ's name. Because *koinonia* is sharing, it has special relevance for ministry evangelism. We share Christ as we give ourselves to others at the point of their need and hurt.

Joyce Coleman was desperate when she came to the Benevolence Center of First Baptist Church, Leesburg, Florida. Struggling to hold back tears, Joyce explained: "I can't pay my rent. I'm going to be evicted, thrown out on the street." The workers at the center helped meet her immediate need by paying her rent. She was also given clean clothing and food.

After some of Joyce's basic needs were met and she was given hope, a worker at the center asked, "Do you know Jesus as your personal Savior?" Joyce hung her head. "Would you like to know Him? With His strength you can persevere through all of your problems." Joyce lifted her eyes and nodded yes. Joyce was then led to commit her life to the Lord Jesus Christ.

Joyce's story illustrates *koinonia* in action. The church gives itself and its love to those in need. Sharing in Christ's love meets human needs and brings persons into saving relationships with Jesus.

God's people. The Old Testament presents Israel as God's special people. Abram, better known to us as Abraham, was called by God to go to a land God would show him. God promised to make him into a great nation and to bless him and those who would come after him. God announced to Abram not only that he would be blessed but also that he would " 'be a blessing' " (Gen. 12:2). So grand would be the mission of those who would descend from Abram that God promised him,

"All peoples on earth
will be blessed through you" (Gen. 12:3).

These promises would find their fulfillment in Israel, God's chosen people.

The Israelites often forgot that their call was to a worldwide redemptive mission. God's prophets repeatedly called the people back to that purpose, but too often they interpreted God's call to them as a call to privilege instead of to ministry. By the time Jesus began His earthly ministry, the mission had been almost forgotten. In its place was a legalistic religious system that excluded more persons than it included. As God's people, Israel had largely failed. Of course, God had sent His written Word through the Jews; and most importantly, He sent Jesus, His living Word, through His people, Israel.

Jesus was often in conflict with the Jewish religious leaders, who were threatened by His fresh approach to a relationship with God. Their opposition to Him grew until it reached a point of no return. Not long before His crucifixion Jesus presented two very pointed parables that enraged them. The first of these is recorded in Matthew 21:28-32:

> "There was a man who had two sons. He went to the first and said, 'Son, go and work today in the vineyard.'
>
> " 'I will not,' he answered, but later he changed his mind and went.
>
> "Then the father went to the other son and said the same thing. He answered, 'I will, sir,' but he did not go.
>
> "Which of the two did what his father wanted?"
>
> "The first," they answered.
>
> Jesus said to them, "I tell you the truth, the tax collectors and the prostitutes are entering the kingdom of God ahead of you. For John came to you to show you the way of righteousness, and you did not believe him, but the tax collectors and the prostitutes did. And even after you saw this, you did not repent and believe him" (Matt. 21:28-32).

For Jesus to say that prostitutes and tax collectors were accepting the way of righteousness, while the religious leaders were not, directly attacked the Jews' supposed position of privilege as God's people. Jesus even stated that such persons were entering God's kingdom ahead of the religious leaders. No wonder they became enraged.

Jesus spoke in even clearer terms in Matthew 21:33-44:

"There was a landowner who planted a vineyard. He put a wall around it, dug a winepress in it and built a watchtower. Then he rented the vineyard to some farmers and went away on a journey. When the harvest time approached, he sent his servants to the tenants to collect his fruit.

"The tenants seized his servants; they beat one, killed another, and stoned a third. Then he sent other servants to them, more than the first time, and the tenants treated them the same way. Last of all, he sent his son to them. 'They will respect my son,' he said.

"But when the tenants saw the son, they said to each other, 'This is the heir. Come, let's kill him and take his inheritance.' So they took him and threw him out of the vineyard and killed him.

"Therefore, when the owner of the vineyard comes, what will he do to those tenants?"

"He will bring those wretches to a wretched end," they replied, "and he will rent the vineyard to other tenants, who will give him his share of the crop at harvest time."

Jesus said to them, "Have you never read in the Scriptures:

" 'The stone the builders rejected
   has become the capstone;
the Lord has done this,
   and it is marvelous in our eyes'?

"Therefore I tell you that the kingdom of God will be taken away from you and given to a people who will produce its fruit. He who falls on this stone will be broken to pieces, but he on whom it falls will be crushed" (Matt. 21:33-44).

Jesus' words that conclude this parable could not be misunderstood. The kingdom would be taken from the legalistic, exclusive institution that Israel had become and " 'given to a people who will produce its fruit' " (Matt. 21:43). Clearly, Jesus announced in this parable God's intention to call to Himself a new, believing people. The Jewish religious leaders knew exactly what Jesus was saying and at this point began their plan to arrest Him (see Matt. 21:45-46).

The New Testament clearly and frequently refers to the church as God's people. Paul wrote: "We are the temple of the living God. As God has said, 'I will live with them and walk among them, and I will be their

God, and they will be my people' " (2 Cor. 6:16). Peter wrote convincingly: "You are a chosen people, a royal priesthood, a holy nation, a people belonging to God, that you may declare the praises of him who called you out of darkness into his wonderful light. Once you were not a people, but now you are the people of God; once you had not received mercy, but now you have received mercy" (1 Pet. 2:9-10). The images used in this passage are powerful and deeply rooted in the promises God made to Israel. The believers to whom Peter wrote and, by implication, all Christians are a chosen people, a royal priesthood, and a holy nation. These are the designations Peter gave to the ordinary, suffering believers to whom he addressed his letter.

Peter reminded his readers, "Once you were not a people, but now you are the people of God" (1 Pet. 2:10). The word translated *people* in this verse is *laos,* the same word Paul used in 2 Corinthians 6:17 to refer to God's people. *Laos* is often translated *laity,* meaning all of the people who believe in Jesus and are committed to Him. The term *God's people* refers to every believer, including pastors and church leaders. All Christians are the *laos* of God.[12]

Christians are God's new people. The church is the new Israel. Every promise and privilege of God's people now belongs to believers in Jesus Christ. In the words of Bill J. Leonard, "the image people of God ... links the church with all God's faithful people throughout time and provides an identity in the divine scheme of things."[13]

Because the church is God's new people, we need to understand why we have been called to be His people. Remember, God's call to Israel was a call to be a blessing, a call to mission. God's call to His people today, church leaders and members, is to do His work in a broken, sinful world. Findley B. Edge went to the heart of what it means to be God's people when he wrote: "God calls the new Israel to be His people, and you and I make the audacious claim that we are a part of this new Israel of God. But the thing we must understand with clarity is, the new Israel is called for precisely the same purpose as was the original Israel. Basic in our call is a call to a task. *We are called to a mission.* "[14]

God's new people are called "a royal priesthood" (1 Pet. 2:9). Martin Luther and other Reformation leaders emphasized the doctrine of the priesthood of believers, reminding the Christian world that every believer is God's priest. They opposed the Roman Catholic Church's idea that insisted on the clergy's role as priests who stood between God and ordinary believers. In Catholic theology of that time laypersons had to approach God through a priest's mediation. Luther and others emphasized that because every believer is a priest, every believer has direct and personal access to God through Jesus Christ, the Great High Priest.

Evangelical Christians also emphasize this understanding of the priesthood of believers. This is certainly a valid understanding of the doctrine, but it is not complete. Findley B. Edge explains the other aspects of this precious doctrine. First, the doctrine of direct access to God means that God is at work in approaching every believer. Christians do not have to depend on others to know that God is speaking to them. We can approach God directly, without human mediation, and God also approaches us directly and personally.

Another implication of our priesthood is every believer's responsibility to discover his or her spiritual gift and to develop that gift for use in ministry. The church has the responsibility to help every member discover and develop spiritual gifts.

The other important implication of the priesthood of believers is that every Christian is a minister. Findley B. Edge recalls his early experiences as the pastor of three small churches when he felt that his job was to do the work of ministry instead of equipping his people to be ministers. His growing understanding of the priesthood of believers led him to conclude that if Christians "could come to understand this doctrine in the fullness of its meaning and if we were to express it in our lives, this doctrine would revolutionize the life and ministry of our churches."[15] Ministry evangelism is a powerful way for Christians to express fully the priesthood of believers.

John, 41 years old, had a superficial religious experience at an early age but was taught that his salvation depended on his ability to meet criteria set by others. John became so discouraged that he gave up, feeling unable to meet the standards and expectations that had been set for him. Finally, conditions became so bad at home that his parents threw him out. At age 14 John was forced to live on the streets of Orlando, where his life became a disaster. Drinking, taking drugs, and associating with a gang became a way of life.

When John was 17, he joined the army; but the conflict inside him would not go away. His drinking continued, and with it came a serious moral decline. John was in jail 15 times. He had many conflicts with the law and numerous fights. Twice he was beaten so badly that he was dragged somewhere and left for dead. Even worse than his physical and social decline was his spiritual emptiness. In his own words, "A part of me longed for fellowship with God, and another part of me said, 'It's no use.' "

When John came to the Rescue Mission of First Baptist Church, Leesburg, Florida, he was a broken man with little hope. At the mission John received the physical help he needed. But more importantly, he was introduced to Jesus Christ and was taught the biblical truths that have set him free and have given him hope and motivation for rebuilding his life.

John explains what the Rescue Mission's ministry has meant to him: "We have a family atmosphere here. The counseling is straight from the Word of God. I've become a member of First Baptist Church of Leesburg, and now I have a place to belong. Through the Rescue Mission my spiritual life is again headed in the right direction, and I feel positive about my life."

John's story is an example of the church, God's people, at work in the world. God's people are priests, who mediate God's love and mercy to lost, hurting persons. When persons like John find hope in Jesus Christ, they too become part of God's people. They too become God's priests, with the privilege of direct contact with God and the responsibility to take His message to others.

The body of Christ. The body of Christ, used as an image of the church, is found several times in Paul's writings. Romans 12:4-5 speaks of the church's unity and diversity, using the image of a body: "Just as each of us has one body with many members, and these members do not all have the same function, so in Christ we who are many form one body, and each member belongs to all the others." Paul addressed the same theme in 1 Corinthians 12: "We were all baptized by one Spirit into one body" (v. 13).

In 1 Corinthians 12:14-26 Paul developed the idea of the interdependence of every part of the body with all other parts. The human body is made up of many parts, but each has a relationship to all other parts of the body: "If one part suffers, every part suffers with it; if one part is honored, every part rejoices with it" (1 Cor. 12:26). All parts of a human body are necessary if someone is to function fully and effectively. All of the parts make up one body. Paul then became more specific: "Now you are the body of Christ, and each one of you is a part of it" (1 Cor. 12:27). Just as various body parts belong to one human body, all of the many, diverse people who have trusted Jesus as Savior and Lord belong to the church, the body of Christ.

The importance of the concept of the body has roots in both Greek and Hebrew thought. First-century Greek thought considered the world one body. Humanity was part of that body. In Hebrew thought, certain individuals were used in a corporate sense to represent all people. For example, Paul used Adam to represent the entire human race when he wrote, "As in Adam all die" (1 Cor. 15:22). The idea is that each person is one with Adam in his sinfulness and in the consequences of that sinfulness. In other words, we share a corporate identity with all humans, the children of Adam. The second half of 1 Corinthians 15:22 says, "So in Christ all will be made alive." Again, the idea of corporate identity is evident. Our identity with Adam brings death, but our identity with Christ brings life. Paul elaborated on this corporate idea in Romans 5:12-22.

The importance of the body of Christ is further seen in the Lord's Supper, the breaking of His body and the shedding of His blood. No doubt the Gospel writers saw a definite connection between individual salvation and the crucified, resurrected body of Jesus.[16]

Probably, all of these ideas are involved in Paul's designation of the church as the body of Christ. The church is God's people, who have been brought together in Christ. Bill J. Leonard writes, "The New Testament image of the body of Christ unites the Hebrew idea of corporate relationship with the Greek concept of body as a unity of various parts."[17]

More clearly than any other image of the church, the body of Christ defines the church's identity. Bill J. Leonard points out the significance of the image of the church as the body of Christ:

• The church does not just represent the body of Christ; it is the body of Christ. "The body of Christ is Christ Himself in direct and intimate relationship with His people."

• The image of the church as the body of Christ involves the essential unity of the church: "all who are united to Christ are united to one another." There is diversity of function, but there is also essential unity in Christ.

• Jesus Christ is the Head of His body, the church (see Eph. 1:22-23; Col. 1:18). As in the human body, every part of Christ's body has a direct relationship to the Head: "Christ's headship gives unity, purpose, and direction to the body."[18]

The image of the church as the body of Christ does not imply that the church is Christ but that there is no church apart from vital union with Jesus. His coming in the flesh is a unique fact of history. The church is not merely a group of persons who meet together to do good things. The church is a body, intimately joined to Christ and to one another.

Although the church is not Christ, it is His body in the world. Because the church must carry on Christ's work in the world, the church, if it is true to its mission, must love persons as He would love them if He were still here in the flesh. The church must touch lives in mercy and love, just as He would do. The church must be forgiving and redemptive, just as He was in His earthly ministry and would be today if He ministered in the flesh. Some have spoken of the church as the continuing incarnation. Just as the eternal Word was made flesh and ministered on this earth, the church must continue His redemptive work and do what He did. Jesus must have had this idea in mind when He said to His disciples: " 'I tell you the truth, anyone who has faith in me will do what I have been doing. He will do even greater things than these, because I am going to the Father' " (John 14:12).

The church is Jesus' body, placed in the world to carry on His ministry of reconciliation under His direction. Being the body of Christ in the world is really what ministry evangelism is all about. It is more than doing good, even from the most humane motives. Ministry evangelism is God's people—His body—carrying on His work in His world.

WHEN THE CHURCH IS REALLY THE CHURCH

H. Stephen Shoemaker in *Strength in Weakness,* his commentary on 2 Corinthians, distinguishes between a theology of glory and a theology of the cross:

> A theology of glory is the theology of super-apostles, a theology without the cross. It says that God is a God of strength who blesses his chosen with power, health, and wealth. Christ's suffering and death had its indispensable place in giving us salvation but has no place in our present way of life. In their formulas: Christ became human that we might become divine, Christ became poor that we might become rich, Christ became powerless that we might have power, Christ suffered that we might escape suffering. ... It thinks it gets its strength from God but in fact feeds off the cultural modes of power.[19]

A theology of the cross represents a stark contrast: "The cross is precisely where we see the essence of God. In the cross we see and know the power and wisdom of God."[20]

Each of these theologies, the theology of glory and the theology of the cross, influences the way a church sees itself. Shoemaker writes: "The theology of glory is the proud posture of a church which locates itself among the 'healthy, wealthy, and wise.' A theology of the cross is the way of the servant-church which serves the world God so loves."[21]

In its search for identity "every church should ask itself: is our ministry located among the well or the sick, among the rich or the poor, among the saved or the lost, among the full or the empty, among the powerful at the center of things or among the powerless and weak on the margins of life? Then we must ask: to whom did Christ come?"[22] This does not mean that an affluent church cannot be an authentic church. "While we may begin our ministry among the well, rich, saved, full, and powerful, our ministry, like that of our Lord, is always self-emptying. ... We spend and are spent for the sake of others."[23]

Every church must find answers to questions about its identity and reason for being. First Baptist Church of Leesburg, Florida, is no exception. This church, founded in 1871, is situated in a small town in central Florida, one of the fastest-growing states in the nation. In 1970 First Baptist had 1,398 members, had an income of almost $100,000, and gave $16,000 to missions causes. At that time the church averaged 370 in Sunday School and had fewer than 20 baptisms a year. All of these statistics are typical of Baptist churches in many small towns.

Today First Baptist Church has almost 6,000 members. The church's annual income is about $2 million, and the church has had over 300 baptisms for each of the past several years. Ministry evangelism is the dynamic that has changed this church. In 1982 the church launched its first ministry, the Rescue Mission for homeless men. Since that time the church has established over 70 ministries, including the Children's Shelter, the Pregnancy-Care Center, and the Women's Care Center. Over the past 10 years the church has acquired 11 pieces of property adjacent to the church to house its many ministries. In 1985 a Christian-Life Center was constructed to house the Child-Development Center and other ministries. New facilities are planned to replace some of the buildings housing the various ministries. When this project is completed, the church will have a ministry campus, including a training facility to aid churches that wish to study ways to minister and evangelize.

The tremendous growth in membership, finances, facilities, and ministries at First Baptist, Leesburg, results directly from the church's response to the questions "To whom does the church belong?" and "What is the church?" Under the leadership of the pastor, this church has discovered and affirmed its reason for being. Members understand that their church is not really theirs—it belongs to Jesus Christ. They continue to discover that their church's purpose is to minister redemptively to persons, to give itself away, truly to be a servant church. For First Baptist this means sharing God's love in practical ways and leading persons to give their hearts to Jesus. Although the church is large in membership, finances, and facilities, everything is built on a theology of the cross. The people, buildings, and resources all belong to Jesus. The church spends itself and gives itself away to a world of suffering, hurt, need, and lostness.

Paula is a 28-year-old single parent. She and her two daughters, Brittany and Jessica, moved to Florida from their home state of Ohio in 1992.

Paula's new job paid well, although she worked 12 hours a day and had little time to spend with Brittany and Jessica.

Everything seemed to be going well for a time. Then things began to fall apart. When Brittany got sick, Paula had to quit her job to take care of her. Bills and expenses continued to mount. Then Paula's relationship with her boyfriend ended. Paula was penniless and had no one to whom she could turn for help. Soon her troubles grew worse when she discovered that she was pregnant. Her self-esteem sank even lower.

Paula and her daughters moved into the Women's Care Center of First Baptist Church of Leesburg in November 1993. Paula spoke of this experience in a testimony at First Baptist Church.

> Being in a Christian home did not impress me in the least. I had asked for help; but I was very rebellious, and that showed on my first night at the center. It was Tuesday, and the church was having a revival. I had to go, but I was going to wear my bib overalls. If no one liked it, that was tough!
>
> The next night I went to the revival service again. As the service ended, I felt the need to give my life to God, but I was fighting. I was afraid to walk up in front of all those people. When my friend noticed that I was crying, she leaned over and said she would go with me. The moment I gave in, I felt a peace around me. I was finally convinced that without the Lord I was not going to make it. That night I gave my life to Jesus.

Since that time Paula has given birth to her third daughter, Cortney Rae. Reflecting on her experience at the Women's Care Center, Paula said: "I went into the Women's Care Center lost, depressed, broke, without friends, angry, bitter, and confused. I left with loving new friends and a great church family. Even though I left my friends at the center behind, I took with me the best friend a person could ever have, and that is Jesus."

Stories like Paula's are often heard from hurting persons whose lives have been healed through loving ministry and a positive witness. Surely, the church is at its best when it reaches out in love to give hope to those who need redemption.

Many churches are not serving and witnessing as the called-out body of Christ in the world. Too often, the church operates in a maintenance mode rather than in a servant mode. Ministry evangelism calls for a return to New Testament concepts of the church. In most congregations this means changing the way we see ourselves and the way we do church. Bill Hull writes,

"For a church to change, it must first experience insight, then pray a prayer of repentance, and finally a prayer of inquiry concerning God's plan for it."[24] These three elements are vital. Insight will come when a church honestly faces what the Bible teaches about the church's nature and purpose. Repentance will follow as the church—leaders and members—face the truth that most of the church's time and resources have been spent on serving the congregation rather than on reaching and touching the lost. Then a prayer of inquiry will rise from the hearts of church members who honestly want to know God's answer to the question, What does God want our church to do to express His love, compassion, and redemptive plan?

The church's call to ministry evangelism is really a call to return to what God has always intended for the church to be. It is a return to the truth that the church's success is measured not so much in numbers as in involvement with persons who need to know that God loves them, no matter what they have done or what their positions are in life. It is recovering the awareness that God is more concerned with what the church does between Sundays than with what happens at church on Sunday.

[1]Bill J. Leonard, *The Nature of the Church*, vol. 12 in *Layman's Library of Christian Doctrine* (Nashville: Broadman Press, 1986), 9.
[2]Walter Shurden, *The Doctrine of the Priesthood of Believers* (Nashville: Convention Press, 1987), 61–62.
[3]Paul Minear, *Images of the Church in the New Testament* (Philadelphia: The Westminster Press, 1960), 17.
[4]Leonard, *The Nature of the Church*, 42.
[5]Trent C. Butler, gen. ed., *Holman Bible Dictionary* (Nashville: Holman Bible Publishers, 1991), 259.
[6]Leonard, *The Nature of the Church*, 42.
[7]Bill Hull, *Can We Save the Evangelical Church?* (Grand Rapids: Revell, 1993), 7.
[8]Ibid., 8.
[9]Leonard, *The Nature of the Church*, 43.
[10]Ibid.
[11]Ibid.
[12]Findley B. Edge, *The Doctrine of the Laity* (Nashville: Convention Press, 1985), 9.
[13]Leonard, *The Nature of the Church*, 45.
[14]Edge, *The Doctrine of the Laity*, 24.
[15]Ibid., 44.
[16]Leonard, *The Nature of the Church*, 46.
[17]Ibid.
[18]Ibid., 46–47.
[19]H. Stephen Shoemaker, *Strength in Weakness* (Nashville: Broadman Press, 1989), 32.
[20]Ibid., 33.
[21]Ibid.
[22]Ibid.
[23]Ibid., 33–34.
[24]Hull, *Can We Save the Evangelical Church?* 17.

4

Ministry to Those Who Minister

HEALTH AND FITNESS are major priorities in our society. You see evidence of this fact everywhere:
• Someone gets up at dawn to run four miles before work.
• Several adults meet daily to walk in a shopping mall.
• The memberships of health clubs and gyms are at an all-time high.
• A group meets weekly for *First Place: A Christ-Centered Health Program*.[1]
• An adult examines the labels of canned and packaged foods to learn the number of fat grams in these products.
• Thousands of people are giving up the deadly habit of smoking and are insisting on smoke-free environments in which to work, dine, and travel.
The reason for all of this? Concern for achieving and maintaining physical health and fitness.

We are concerned not only about nutrition and exercise to maintain good health but also about medical and surgical care to restore health. Modern medicine offers the finest medical and surgical services ever known. Medicines can conquer once hopeless diseases. Medical care is important for the same reason we consider exercise and nutrition important—we want to keep our bodies healthy and functioning.

Concern about physical health and well-being is legitimate. If we take care of our bodies, we look better, feel better, live longer, and function more efficiently. For a Christian, caring for the body is a sacred responsibility because our bodies are temples of the Holy Spirit. We belong to Him physically and spiritually because He has bought us (see 1 Cor. 6:19-20).

Just as concern for the physical body is important, so is concern for the health and fitness of Jesus' body, the church. We have previously seen that the most accurate description of the New Testament church is the body of Christ. Just as the human body is interdependent, with every body part dependent on all other parts, every church member is a part of the body of Christ and is dependent on all other parts (see 1 Cor. 12:25). The human body cannot function effectively if any part of it is hurt or is not well. For example, maybe you can recall a time when a toothache brought you to a halt physically, even though you were healthy in every other way. In the same way, the body of Christ, the church, cannot function effectively if any part of it, any member, is hurt or broken. This is why in the church, as in the human body, each part of the body must take care of all other parts of the body (see 1 Cor. 12:25-26).

As we have seen, God has given His church tremendous tasks to perform. He wants His church to reach and disciple all people (see Matt. 28:18) and to respond to the world's hurts and brokenness through caring ministry. Because we are the body of Christ in the world, God depends on us to perform the tasks of evangelism and ministry, which require a high level of commitment and abundant energy. To do this work effectively, the body of Christ must be healthy and strong.

Just as the human body is maintained by food, rest, exercise, and a healthy attitude, the body of Christ must have certain elements that promote health in order to carry out God's work in the world. This is especially true if a church responds to God's call to ministry evangelism. Ministry involvement with hurting persons requires a healthy church. In this chapter we will focus on ways to build up and maintain a strong body of Christ that can meet the demands of ongoing, compassionate ministry to the world.

FELLOWSHIP IN GOD'S FAMILY

The church can minister in the world only if it functions in an atmosphere of mutual caring. The believers who made up the earliest church really cared about one another. Luke wrote about this early church, "They devoted themselves to the apostles' teaching and to the fellowship, to the breaking of bread and to prayer" (Acts 2:42). They "had everything in common," even selling their personal property to meet the needs of other members of the group (see Acts 2:44-45). They met together on a regular basis; took the Lord's Supper together; and enjoyed one another's company in simple ways, such as eating together (see Acts 2:46). These activities present a picture of strong, sustaining love that formed the context in which these believers carried on their ministry. The Greek word *koinonia* describes what these believers experienced (see Acts 2:42).

Koinonia, translated *fellowship* in our Bibles, is the characteristic environment of the New Testament church. *Fellowship*, however, is not an adequate translation of *koinonia*. The word *fellowship* is sometimes used to describe a casual, friendly, cordial relationship among persons. *Koinonia* means much more. It refers to sharing life. Fellowship can occur on a surface level. *Koinonia* is a deep sense of belonging to one another.

Christian fellowship is a miracle from God. It cannot be manufactured or orchestrated artificially. John put it this way: "We proclaim to you what we have seen and heard so that you may have fellowship with us. And our fellowship is with the Father and with his Son, Jesus Christ" (1 John 1:3).

Paul closed his second letter to the Corinthian church with the prayer that "the fellowship of the Holy Spirit be with you all" (2 Cor. 13:14). Christian fellowship (*koinonia*) is not just among Christians. It involves the Father, Son, and Holy Spirit. Fellowship, in the biblical sense, includes the interaction between believer and believer and between the Lord and believers. This is the reason fellowship cannot be created. God gives it to His people.

The miracle of *koinonia* is realized in the context of the body of Christ. Christians can truly share life because each one is a part of Christ's body (see 1 Cor. 12:27). The idea that one part of the human body would work against another part is ludicrous. Because each body part is part of the whole body, the various members of the body work together. They need one another, support one another, and take care of one another. In other words, the human body functions in unity. So it is with the body of Christ.

When the body of Christ, the church, is healthy, it works together. Every church member is needed and is important. Every member shares life with all other members. The church has great diversity but also enjoys unity (see 1 Cor. 12:12-27). This is what *koinonia* is all about. The fellowship of believers with the Lord and with one another transcends differences. Life in the church of the Lord Jesus is shared life. Ken Hemphill writes: "In Christ, we actually become one body, so much so that we feel one another's pain and joy. When we stub our toes, and it hurts, our whole body feels the pain. When one of our members experiences pain and weeps, we should all weep. The idea here is that we actually stand beside one another in fellowship so much that we feel the pain and experience the joy."[2] If God's people are to witness and minister to a lost and hurting world, *koinonia* must be the sustaining context in which they find their strength and will to do so.

The church is sometimes described as a family or a household. Paul advised Timothy, "If I am delayed, you will know how people ought to conduct themselves in God's household, which is the church of the living God, the pillar and foundation of the truth" (1 Tim. 3:15). God is revealed in the New Testament as the Father of the family. Significantly, a word Jesus frequently used for *Father* is the Aramaic word *Abba* (see Matt. 6:9). Paul said that we are able to address God as *Abba* through Jesus Christ (see Rom. 8:15). The word *Abba* is the tender family word a child would use to address his father. The nearest equivalent to *Abba* in our language is *Daddy*. Believers are called children of God (see 1 John 3:2). Jesus is identified as a believer's brother (see Heb. 2:11). Christians relate to one another as fathers, mothers, brothers, and sisters (see 1 Tim. 5:1-2). All of these relationships suggest family. The church is God's family.

Christians sometimes give lip service to the idea of the church as family without realizing what this implies. The family relationships among Christians are spiritual in nature rather than natural or physical. We recognize the importance of earthly family relationships. Spiritually, God's family, the church, provides the appropriate environment and relationships for developing a witnessing, ministering life. The following qualities describe the way a church supports and ministers to its members.

Acceptance. In a family that seeks to honor God, we find unconditional acceptance, not rejection, censure, and injustice. Even when we fail or other family members are shocked, disappointed, or grieved by what we have done, they continue to offer us love and acceptance. At its best, the church is a spiritual family in which individual Christians find acceptance. This does not mean that the family always approves but that every believer can find love and acceptance at his best or worst.

Forgiveness. Closely related to acceptance in a family is forgiveness. A family forgives a family member, even when he has caused embarrassment or pain. The same must be true in God's family if the family is to function according to His plan. Peter probably thought he was being very generous when he asked Jesus: " 'Lord, how many times shall I forgive my brother when he sins against me? Up to seven times?' " (Matt. 18:21). Forgiving seven times was much more than the law required. But Jesus replied, " 'I tell you, not seven times, but seventy-seven times' " (Matt. 18:22). Even this number was obviously not meant to suggest a limitation on forgiveness. The idea is that forgiveness is unlimited in God's family. Paul put in perspective the matter of forgiveness in God's family when he wrote, "Forgive as the Lord forgave you" (Col. 3:13). The church is the fellowship of the forgiven. In light of God's mercy, Christians must practice forgiveness in God's family.

Sharing. Healthy families share both good and bad experiences. Births and deaths, joys and sorrows, successes and failures, laughter and tears—all are shared in a loving family. That family cares about the ups and downs, celebrations and disappointments of each family member.

When Paul described the church as the body of Christ, with each Christian being a part of the body, he said, "If one part suffers, every part suffers with it; if one part is honored, every part rejoices with it" (1 Cor.

12:26). In God's family, experiences must be felt and shared by the entire family.

A church experienced tremendous trauma when the husband of one member shot himself on the church steps. He died there, leaving a widow and a church family stunned and grieving. The next several days were difficult for everyone; but the church members proved their character, giving sincere love to the widow and support to one another.

When the pastor stood before the people on the Sunday after the tragedy, he put aside the sermon he had planned, instead providing a time for members to process their feelings. The pastor pointed out that one lesson to be learned from the tragedy was that the church must be a family in which all share with compassion the experiences of individual members. Just as important, the pastor insisted, is that the church family share members' ordinary experiences, such as the death of a loved one, the loss of a job, and the birth of a child. God's family should care about and share family members' joys and sorrows.

Nurture. The word *nurture* probably best describes the atmosphere in healthy families. Family members' love for one another causes them to build up, encourage, and enable other family members. That is why family life is so valuable to the development of healthy, happy individuals.

God's family should also nurture its members. Every family member is important. Each has unrealized potential. Each has gifts to offer. The church family's role is to encourage and enable all members to discover and use their gifts and experience the joy of Christian growth.

Only in the *koinonia* of God's family, the church, can individuals become what God intends for them to be. We often hear families described as dysfunctional, meaning that the family is not working properly. Perhaps love, trust, and affirmation are missing. In some cases abuse and cruelty have made the family a destructive influence. Sadly, God's family can also become dysfunctional. Pride, self-seeking, anger, bitterness, and other negative forces can change the church from the nurturing family God intended to a stumbling block to growth and ministry. By God's grace we must not let God's family be weakened or destroyed. Only when a church provides a loving, accepting, nurturing atmosphere for its members can they develop the qualities and skills needed to minister and witness effectively to a broken world.

THE CHALLENGE TO DEVELOP DISCIPLES

The basketball team of a leading university found itself in a difficult position. Because of a change in the coaching staff, several players left the team before the season began. Other players quit during the season. Because the coaching staff was new, it did not have time to recruit additional quality players. Consequently, the team played that season with only eight players on the squad. When two players sustained injuries, the team had only six players for several games. Although the team played hard and gave its best effort throughout the season, it could remain competitive for about 75 percent of the game. Then as fatigue set in, turnovers and other mistakes increased. By the middle of the second half, the team had no more to give.

Sadly, this understaffed basketball team is a picture of many churches. A recent study by Bobby Eklund indicates that from 12 to 16 percent of Baptist church members give 80 cents of each dollar given.[3] What is true of giving is undoubtedly true of every area of church participation. A relatively small percentage of members provides most of the leadership and ministry in most congregations. Like the basketball team with too few players, most churches limp along because a few members are trying to do so much. When this is the case, the body of Christ is crippled and fatigued. Those who are trying to do all of the work become burned-out and discouraged. When this happens, ministry evangelism is virtually impossible. Winning persons to Jesus through caring ministry requires a functioning body with a high degree of involvement.

Statistics for the past several years paint a troubling picture. At least one-half of all members of Southern Baptist churches are classified as inactive, meaning that these persons have not attended for at least one year. Therefore, only about 50 percent of Southern Baptist church members can be considered active by any definition. When we consider that *active* is defined as *attending a church service once in 12 months,* the picture worsens. Obviously, many of these "active" members are not truly involved in the church's life and ministry. In too many churches the body of Christ cannot function because it is crippled by parts of the body that are inactive.

What has created the problem of uninvolved and inactive church members? A major cause is a misunderstanding of the Great Commission. When Jesus gave this command to His disciples, He said: " 'Go and make disciples of all nations' " (Matt. 28:19). The command is not to make converts but to make disciples. The difference between the two is significant. Many churches are effective in making converts but not very good at making disciples. Of course, individuals must be converts before they can be disciples. The experience of trusting in the Lord Jesus Christ for salvation is indispensable. Evangelical Christians believe in the absolute necessity of the salvation experience. But something is wrong with evangelism that does not result in discipleship.

Discipleship describes the ongoing nature of the Christian life. Disciples are followers of Jesus. Disciples are pupils. They are learning, growing, developing believers. Disciples are becoming more like Jesus in love, attitudes, and actions. Disciples are serious Christians who are growing "in the grace and knowledge of our Lord and Savior Jesus Christ" (2 Pet. 3:18). Disciples are not perfect, but they are becoming what they were saved to be—vital, functioning parts of the body of Christ.

Ministry evangelism requires disciples. Only disciples can understand God's heart for hurting persons. Only disciples can be trained, equipped, and willing to use their spiritual gifts to minister and win others to faith in Christ.

If the body of Christ is healthy, its first concern should be developing disciples. This disciple-building process must begin as soon as a person decides to accept Christ as Savior and must continue throughout the believer's life. The process of disciple making never ends.

Although the new birth can be considered an event, discipleship must be regarded as a process. Discipleship is closely related to the biblical doctrine of sanctification. The word *sanctify* means *set apart*. This setting apart begins with the initial salvation experience. Paul wrote to the Corinthian believers, "You were washed, you were sanctified, you were justified in the name of the Lord Jesus Christ and by the Spirit of our God" (1 Cor. 6:11). Positionally, Christians are set apart or sanctified by God at the moment of their salvation. However, another important dimension to sanctification is that God wants us to be sanctified experientially. Paul expressed this dimension of sanctification when he prayed for his friends at Thessalonica: "May God himself, the God of peace, sanctify you through and through" (1 Thess. 5:23). Being sanctified "through and through" describes ongoing action. The Christian *has been* sanctified and *is being* sanctified as an ongoing experience. This ongoing sanctification occurs in discipleship. *Discipleship* refers to the human side of this process; *sanctification,* to the divine side. A Christian follows Jesus in discipleship. As the disciple follows the Lord, the Holy Spirit carries out the process of sanctification. Sanctification, like discipleship, is an ongoing process, never finished on this side of heaven.

Ultimately, developing a disciple is the Holy Spirit's work. However, God's work in the individual's life involves human cooperation. The believer must want to grow and develop in discipleship, and the church must provide opportunities for discipleship.

The leaders of First Baptist Church, Leesburg, Florida, understand the importance of discipleship to ministry evangelism. After persons commit their lives to Jesus Christ, the church provides tools to help them develop as disciples. Years of experience in ministry evangelism have revealed that as a person's relationship with God deepens, that person will become involved in ministry and will be open to God's use in winning others to Christ. The transition from spiritual infancy to maturity requires time, but the process must begin immediately for a new Christian and must continue until God shapes the Christian in accordance with His purpose. Therefore, First Baptist, Leesburg, has established a discipleship process that includes basic Christian training following conversion, training in discovering and developing spiritual gifts, and training and support for ministering Christians.

No matter how your church structures its discipleship process, certain elements are essential to any meaningful disciple-making program. We will examine the steps necessary to help Christians grow as disciples.

Assimilation of new Christians. New Christians' assimilation into the church's fellowship is necessary if they are to grow as Jesus' disciples. Studies reveal that infants require early bonding to develop properly. For this reason, they need to be held, cuddled, and talked to. New believers also need time to bond with their church family.

A young couple walked down the aisle of a church to make decisions for Christ. Everyone in the church family was happy that they joined, but from the beginning they did not seem to fit in. Because they were shy and did not make friends easily, the church members soon stopped making efforts to involve them in the life of the church. Six months later the couple had become totally inactive.

This story is all too familiar. If new Christians do not connect meaningfully with church members soon after making decisions for Christ, they likely become sporadic in participation or drop out altogether. The two most common reasons persons give for dropping out of church are the lack of care and the lack of friends. Like babies, new Christians must have loving early experiences in the family and must feel that they belong. Without this early assimilation they will not become participating members of the body of Christ.

At First Baptist, Leesburg, this assimilation takes place intentionally, with basic Christian training beginning immediately. New church members are required to participate in a three-session orientation seminar, which introduces them to basic Christian beliefs and to their church leaders. This seminar helps them feel that they are part of the church as they learn about its programs, ministries, and facilities.

The task of assimilating new members does not end with the three-session seminar. Next the assimilation secretary assigns new members to sponsors, to whom they are introduced at the seminar's final session. These sponsors serve as friends and encouragers to the new members for the first six months of membership. In addition, the assimilation secretary tracks the new members' attendance and calls them periodically during the first year of membership. If the situation requires further attention, the assimilation secretary assigns visits from a deacon, a Sunday School teacher, or a staff member.

Not every church provides the thorough, intensive help that First Baptist offers its new members, but every church must take new-member assimilation seriously if its new Christians are to becoming growing disciples. No period in a Christian's life is more crucial than the early days of the Christian experience. Whatever plan a church adopts to assimilate new members, it should include the following elements.

The first essential element in assimilating new church members is appropriate attention at the time they make their decisions to become Christians. New believers should have the benefit of counseling at the time of their decisions. Often, persons come forward during the invitation to make decisions that will affect their lives for eternity; but the church gives little or no opportunity for them to express themselves and to receive biblical instruction about these decisions. Some churches train counselors to help persons at the point of the decision. These churches have established counseling areas, where those making decisions can be counseled, instructed, and prayed with individually. Counselors can be trained by using the four-session training plan found in *Commitment Counseling Manual.* More extensive training can be provided by using the Lay Institute for Equipping (LIFE®) course *DecisionTime: Commitment Counseling.*

After persons have made decisions for Christ and have been counseled, many churches give them copies of *Welcome to God's Family,* a tract that presents basic, immediate information they need to know, such as assurance of salvation, steps to begin spiritual growth, and the importance of baptism and church membership.

It is extremely important that new Christians begin immediately to learn more about the Christian life and to grow as Jesus' disciples. *Survival Kit for Christians* is a valuable tool that helps new Christians understand the meaning of new life in Christ and establish lifelong habits of Christian behavior and growth. The best way to use *Survival Kit* is as a part of the Encourager Plan for New Christians. This plan establishes a partnership between a new Christian and an experienced Christian, who encourages the new believer in the early weeks of his new life in Christ and helps him complete *Survival Kit*. Encouragers can be trained with a one-session training plan available from the Discipleship and Family Leadership Department; the Sunday School Board of the Southern Baptist Convention; 127 Ninth Avenue, North; Nashville, TN 37234. The Encourager Plan for New Christians is especially effective in assimilating new Christians because it combines instruction in the basics of the Christian life with the personal friendship and attention that are essential if a new believer is to grow in discipleship.

The process of assimilating new members into the church and of starting them on the road to becoming mature disciples also involves the Sunday School. Each new church member should immediately be assigned to a Sunday School class. A Sunday School class teaches God's Word, ministers in times of need, and provides a group of Christian friends for love, encouragement, and support. New Christians are much more likely to develop in discipleship if they become active participants in Sunday School.

Before Larry came to the Rescue Mission of First Baptist Church, Leesburg, he had never had a relationship with Jesus, although he had always believed in God. What has happened in his life since he met Christ illustrates the way a church can assimilate a new believer into the fellowship of the body of Christ. Larry's words say it best:

> The Bible study on Tuesday night and the Sunday School lessons are showing me the way to a new life in Christ. Fellowship with others brings the understanding of how to live a clean and healthy life. My growth is not spiritual perfection, and my relationship with Jesus is not performance-based. I have learned a lot about Jesus, His teachings, and how to apply them to my life. I'm not perfect and can grow only as the Holy Spirit leads me. The way I feel is that I have a new lease on life as long as I stay with the Lord.

Training in Christian living. First Baptist Church, Leesburg, does not stop with assimilating new members. Pastor Charles Roesel speaks of a five-fold surrender to the lordship of Christ, which should be every Christian's goal:
1. The mind surrendered to be an intelligent Christian
2. The heart surrendered to be a loving Christian
3. The body surrendered to be a useful Christian
4. The spirit surrendered to be a dynamic Christian
5. The will surrendered to be an obedient Christian

This fivefold surrender describes mature discipleship. Such a level of discipleship does not happen automatically. The Holy Spirit works through the church to develop Christian disciples for ministry in the body of Christ.

After new members have completed the orientation seminar at First Baptist, they can enter one of several discipleship courses offered to help them continue to grow. One course offered at First Baptist, "Beginning Your Christian Walk," was designed especially for new Christians. This course teaches basic Christian principles and equips new believers to handle life's struggles, study the Bible, and develop a prayer life.

When Christians are ready to move to a deeper level, they enroll in "Maturing in Your Christian Walk," a course that focuses on developing a life led by the Spirit of God. After members have completed this course, they can join groups studying various topics such as witnessing, prayer, marriage enrichment, parenting, financial planning, and inductive Bible study.

The next level of courses is called "Serving Christ in the World." These courses are designed to help growing Christians find avenues of service. Specific seminars at this level are "Discovering Your Place of Service in the First Family," "Defending Your Faith," "Advanced Witness Training," "Counseling Basics," and "Spiritual-Gifts Seminar." In addition, courses at this level are offered in advanced leadership for all church leaders, as well as ministry leadership for ministry coordinators and directors. The pastor also leads a seminar every six or eight weeks for all church members who serve in ministries offered by First Baptist Church. This seminar features motivation, ministry training, and encouragement.

Discipleship seminars at First Baptist, Leesburg, meet on Sunday and Wednesday evenings. Lasting from four to eight weeks, they feature training at all levels of Christian maturity and utilize discipleship materials published by the Sunday School Board of the Southern Baptist Convention. Because the courses center on group discussion and participation, the groups are kept small for optimal learning and therefore require preregistration. An attractive booklet lists all available courses, with the dates they will be offered, the names of the leaders, brief course descriptions, and registration information. This booklet is distributed to church members, who are encouraged to use the information to plan their discipleship training.

Churches such as First Baptist, Leesburg, and many others have developed well-planned programs to give their members good beginnings in the Christian faith and encouragement to grow in discipleship toward maturity and service. Many other churches have not yet developed a complete discipleship plan. However, churches of any size can take important steps to promote the growth of their disciples:

1. Every church can take seriously the decision of every new member by providing counseling, instruction, and prayer at the time of decision.
2. Every church can use tools like *Survival Kit for Christians* to provide initial training for persons who have made decisions for Christ.
3. Every church can use a plan like the Encourager Plan for New Christians to assign new Christians to more experienced Christians, who can provide the support and encouragement new believers need.
4. Every church can enroll new Christians and other new members in Sunday School classes, in which they can grow in fellowship with other Christians.
5. Every church can provide general training in discipleship by using such resources as *Baptist Adults*, Baptist Doctrine Study materials, Everyday Discipleship courses, and other short-term courses. Groups of Christians can use these resources to study biblical truths and discipleship responsibilities.
6. Every church can offer in-depth studies in areas such as Bible study, marriage, parenting, witnessing, finding and doing God's will, and prayer. Numerous LIFE® courses are available that involve participants in daily study and group sharing, helping Christians grow in their faith and ministry.
7. Every church can provide specialized training for those who want to learn how to minister more effectively. For example, a church can provide training for its deacons in ministering to church families or witness training for those who want to learn to witness more effectively.
8. Every church can provide worship experiences in which the Word of God is preached and worshipers participate through music, prayer, and fellowship.
9. Every church can cultivate a warm, encouraging fellowship in which believers celebrate together, weep together, and share with one another in Christian *koinonia*.

Developing disciples in Christian living is not optional. Any church that is serious about winning persons to Christ and about ministering to their needs must help its members grow strong as disciples. Equipping believers for ministry is the main task of a church's God-called staff leaders (see Eph. 4:11-12). If pastors and other leaders fail to build disciples, the church will fail to be a ministering, witnessing church.

As directors of the Rescue Mission at First Baptist Church in Leesburg, Joan and Dave McCullen have ministered to scores of men who have fallen into the traps of alcoholism, drug addiction, and homelessness. Many of these men have been won to Christ and are sober, productive citizens. Some of these men have remained in Leesburg and are active at First Baptist.

Joan told the story of a successful businessman who made a career change that proved to be unfulfilling. He turned to alcohol and soon began a downward spiral to a wasted life. Impoverished and discouraged, he came to the mission. He stayed a short while, left, and returned again. Dave shared the truth of the gospel with him—truth with the power to turn his life around. But the man rejected the message. He left the mission again, saying that Joan and Dave had nothing to offer that he wanted.

Joan was standing in the mission's kitchen one day about a year later when she heard someone sobbing at the door. When she went to the door, she found the same man, totally broken. He said that his life had not been satisfying and he had not been able to forget what Dave had shared with him and the sermons the pastor had preached. Overwhelmed by conviction, he had returned to the mission because it was the only home he had.

A place was found for the man to become sober. Once again Dave shared the gospel with him. This time he was receptive and asked Jesus to come into his life. A short while later he was baptized. Now he and his wife serve the Lord together at First Baptist Church.

When the church is willing to develop disciples like Joan and Dave Mc-Cullen, the Holy Spirit can use them in powerful ways to witness and minister to others.

HEALING THE HURTING MEMBERS OF THE BODY

Churches are filled with the walking wounded. The dimensions of our culture's brokenness and hurt are too staggering to believe. Consider the following statistics.

- Half of all marriages in the United States end in divorce. This is the highest divorce rate in the world.
- One in four children now lives in a single-parent home. One in two will live in a single-parent home by the time the child graduates from high school.
- In the past 30 years the suicide rate has tripled. Suicide is the third-highest killer of teenagers.
- One in three girls and one in four boys are sexually abused by age 18.
- A leading magazine reports that incest touches one in five Americans.
- Eleven million people in the United States are alcoholics. This problem affects 76 million family members.
- Between 40 and 80 million Americans are compulsive overeaters.

- Approximately 33.6 million Americans live in poverty, representing 13.5 percent of our population.
- About 9 million people were unemployed at any given time during a recent year.
- About 725,000 bankruptcies were filed in a recent year.
- An estimated 12 million people in this country are workaholics, and the number is rising.[4]

Although we might like to believe that Christians are immune to society's problems and hurts, honesty forces us to admit that our churches are filled with hurting persons. These persons are members of Christ's body, but they are not well. Because of their hurts and problems they are not able to function effectively in the body. This means that the church's ministry suffers because an unhealthy body cannot be a fully functioning body.

Most of the time we are able to deal with our problems, move past them, and go on with our lives. At times, however, a Christian is so wounded or troubled that the pain does not go away without help. The following true story describes the deep pain that some Christians experience. A young woman slipped the following letter into her pastor's hand at the close of a Sunday-morning worship service.

I walked into church last Sunday night hopeful, believing, disbelieving, happy, scared. I prayed that God would give me an answer if He was really listening to me. I needed an answer that night. When it was almost time for the service to be over, my thoughts were: *This isn't for me. God can't answer me.* But when you told a story about a man you knew in Texas whose life had been in shambles but had been reclaimed by the power of Christ, I was deeply touched.

When the people of the church see me, they see a wife, a mother of three children, and a successful professional. What they do not see is the woman who grew up in a Baptist church; whose father was a deacon, Sunday School teacher, and city councilman; and whose mother was active in church and the owner of a day-care center. They see me coming from a "great" family of strong Christians. Yet they do not know that I grew up in a home where beatings were regular for a small girl and where broken bones and scars from cuts and burns were a way of life. Nor can they see the little girl who became the sexual pawn of both parents—mother as well as father. They cannot see the woman who became an alcoholic, a drug addict, and a lady of the streets. They cannot see the woman who totally blacked out her childhood and, only after being raped twice as an adult, finally had the floodgates opened and memories of the lost years recovered. They do not see the person who went through weekly therapy just to make it through each day.

I want to know if there is a place for me in my church. I want to know if the people sitting in the congregation want to know what life can sometimes be. Are they really willing to look and hear? Are they willing to open their arms, or is it just too hard to listen, too X-rated to know or believe? Are some people just too sinful to become clean?

Many persons, like this woman, carry deep scars from life. Others suffer from hurts that impair and disable their spiritual lives. The bereaved, the divorced, the lonely, the person who has lost a job, the brokenhearted—all of these and many more sit in our pews every Sunday. Christians face broken marriages, grief, problems with children, business failures, emotional problems, and broken dreams. Often, circumstances such as retirement, illness, and caring for older parents leave Christians shaken and needy. Sometimes their pain is known; sometimes it is carried silently. These are God's people. They know Him and love Him; but they are wounded and limping physically, emotionally, or spiritually.

If the church is serious about ministry, it must learn to minister to the hurts within the body of Christ—the church. Christians must be trained, equipped, encouraged, ministered to, and emotionally healed if they are to complete the tasks our Lord has assigned. Christians need a church environment in which they can grow spiritually, discover their gifts, and be equipped for ministry. Unless a church recognizes all of these needs and helps its members cope with them, God's army in the world will be a crippled army at best.

Johnny Jones writes: "The church is called by God to be a healing environment. The church is not buildings, bulletins, budgets, and business. It's people—God's people meeting needs."[5] Jones further insists: "We believe our churches must change. We must welcome the broken, oppressed, captive, and blind. We must become a 'hospital' for the broken instead of a 'country club' for the well."[6]

Many churches seek to minister to their hurting members in their times of need. This ministry is important because wounded and needy members who have found love and healing in the body of Christ can then help others find healing. One of the most effective ways a church can become an agent of healing to its members is to offer small-group studies that address specific needs. These discovery groups and support groups provide an environment in which change and healing can take place.

Discovery groups. Discovery groups study problems that individuals face. The group leader guides participants to discuss contemporary life issues such as self-worth and the ways families function. Discovery groups focus on exploring the causes of and solutions to life's problems. These groups are offered for anyone who wishes to grow in understanding a particular subject. An excellent resource for discovery groups is *Search for Significance* LIFE® Support Group Series Edition. This course helps participants develop a thorough understanding of Christian self-esteem and become sensitive to others' hurts and needs. In this way, *Search for Significance* can serve as an entry point to a support-group ministry. Other discovery-group resources are listed in appendix 3.

Support groups. Support groups are composed of persons who meet to deal with issues they hold in common. A support group allows participants to gain awareness, understanding, and support in dealing with personal problems. Support groups exist in most communities, and many of these are very helpful. However, many of these groups do not deal with the spiritual dimensions of life's issues. For a Christian any lasting solution to problems must find its basis in the gospel of Jesus Christ and in the believer's relationship with Him. LIFE® Support Group Series resources, published by the Sunday School Board of the Southern Baptist Convention, provide the best support-group resources that are Christ-centered and biblical in approach. Appendix 3 lists available support-group resources in this series.

LIFE® Support Group Series materials are designed for three types of support groups:
• In *encouragement-and-accountability support groups* members help one another work toward a common goal. An example of this type of support group may be found in the many churches that are using *First Place: A Christ-Centered Health Program.* Through these groups Christians enjoy better health through good nutrition, exercise, and spiritual enrichment.
• *Personal-issues support groups* provide a safe, loving environment in which members can share responses to personal issues. These groups promote spiritual healing and growth as they help members begin to recover from deep hurts and dysfunction in their lives. One popular resource for this type of support group is *Making Peace with Your Past,* which helps adults handle problems that have resulted from growing up in dysfunctional families. Personal-issues support groups may also be organized around

such issues as divorce recovery and grief, and LIFE® Support Group Series resources are provided for addressing these issues, as well. As increasing numbers of Christians confront problems like these, a caring church can offer hope and healing in Christ.

• Every church has members who deal with or fail to deal with problems like alcoholism, drug addiction, eating disorders, sexual addiction, and codependency. The LIFE® Support Group Series provides resources for *12-step recovery groups.* The 12-step approach to recovery, made famous by the work of Alcoholics Anonymous, is adapted in LIFE® Support Group Series products to emphasize recovery through repentance, trust in God, and spiritual renewal. These groups are built on the truth that Jesus Christ is the ultimate and only solution to addiction. Unlike some other approaches to these problems, these support groups are Christ-centered.

The growth of support groups in churches has been dramatic as more and more people in our society struggle with such addictive behaviors as chemical dependency, codependency, anorexia, bulimia, compulsive overeating, and sexual addiction. Many others deal with problems that are not personal addictions but seriously affect their lives. These problems include sexual abuse, bereavement, divorce, rape, incest, losing jobs, caring for aging parents, and depression.

Support groups do not replace professional counseling or therapy. No claims are made for cures. They are, instead, what the name implies—a supportive, safe, and loving environment in which participants can support one another as they cope with hurts and problems.

Churches that want to help their members by offering support groups will want to move carefully into this ministry. After a pastor and other leaders become convinced that these ministries are needed, a support-group coordinator should be selected. This person works with the pastor to select leaders for discovery groups and facilitators for support groups. These leaders and facilitators may be persons who have experienced problems of their own and have found help in a Christ-centered recovery process.

In the LIFE® Support Group Series *LIFE® Support Leader's Handbook* provides training processes for leaders and facilitators. Persons enlisted to work in discovery and support groups will also find valuable help in *Wise-Counsel: Skills for Lay Counseling,* a LIFE® course that helps laypersons develop listening-and-counseling skills.

Churches are encouraged to begin with discovery groups, then to add support groups. Discovery groups will help interested Christians deal with their own needs and become sensitive to issues others face. As discovery groups work through the resources, the need for various support groups will emerge. Guidance for planning and implementing support-group ministries is found in *LIFE® Support Leader's Handbook.*

A church that decides to minister to hurting persons through discovery and support groups will not view these groups as replacing the church's regular worship-and-study activities. These are essential, proven elements of a well-rounded, healthy church. Nor will the groups be seen as permanent. Some will need to last longer than others, but all will work toward the goal of helping hurting perons move through the process of recovery into the church's discipleship ministry.

Saundra Killough and several other members of Hunter's Glen Baptist Church in Plano, Texas, believed that their church needed to do more to meet members' specific needs. Their rapidly growing church was doing a good job of reaching persons but did not offer much discipleship training. Kim Hall, the pastor, responded to this need by asking Saundra to serve as LIFE® ministry coordinator to lead in developing a plan to meet the congregation's specific needs through a program of discipleship training.

Saundra felt a strong sense of calling to her newly assigned task. Her first step was to participate in LIFE® Support Group Series training, led by the LIFE® Support Group Series consultant at the Sunday School Board of the Southern Baptist Convention.

Saundra's next step was to educate church leaders about LIFE® and LIFE® Support Group Series training. Some training had already begun, for the church had offered *Experiencing God: Knowing and Doing the Will of God* and *Search for Significance;* but no ongoing training was offered. The only ongoing activity on Sunday night was the evening worship service. Saundra convinced leaders that the church needed to make relevant training opportunities available to members. They decided to use Sunday nights in an exciting new way by offering tracks of discipleship studies for 12-week periods twice a year that would replace the traditional evening worship service. These tracks would feature small-group studies of life issues that church members faced. Emphasis would also be placed on ministry skills. The track plan would offer group studies for children and youth as well as adults.

Church leaders knew that this concept could succeed only if potential leaders were trained to lead the groups. Workers were enlisted to complete group studies of *LIFE® Support Leader's Handbook* and *WiseCounsel: Skills for Lay Counseling.*

The study-track plan of Hunter's Glen Baptist Church is now in its second year. Small-group studies on life issues such as marriage, parenting, money management, codependency, and Bible study have been offered.

Experiencing God: Knowing and Doing the Will of God and a study of major religions have been offered to the youth group. Children have had study opportunities, too. Each week's session lasts for 1½ hours. At the midpoint of the 12-week track each group takes a break, and a joint celebration service is held. Then the tracks continue. Because the study tracks use LIFE® and LIFE® Support Group Series courses, which require daily work and group accountability, the pastor also leads courses requiring less time and study for those who prefer them. *First Place: A Christ-Centered Health Program* groups are also offered on weekdays. When a 12-week study track ends, evening worship services resume until the next 12-week track begins.

The discipleship-training program at Hunter's Glen has only begun. As leaders are trained and as spiritual gifts are discovered and developed, Saundra Killough looks forward to the time when the church can offer 12-step programs for persons in the church and the community who struggle with addictions.

Not every church will feel led to develop a program of support groups that is as innovative and complete as that of Hunter's Glen Baptist Church; but every church that is serious about ministry must address the needs of its members, especially those who hurt or need help in specific areas of their lives. Only if these needs are addressed and met will a church become a healthy body that is equipped to reach out to those in the world who are lost and broken.

MEETING EVERYDAY NEEDS

Not all church members struggle with dysfunction; yet they still have needs that occasionally arise, such as the loss of a loved one or a job, an illness, marriage-and-family problems, and the complications of aging. If a church is to be strong enough to reach and minister to persons outside the church family, it must also meet its members' everyday needs.

Many ongoing needs for ministry in the body of Christ are routinely met in most churches by pastors, staff members, and other church leaders, who regularly visit hospitals, minister to the bereaved, and listen to persons experiencing problems. In addition to these efforts, First Baptist Church, Leesburg, provides a wide range of ministries that meet church members' needs. Many times needs are not met because church members hesitate to make them known, not wanting to appear vulnerable to fellow church members. First Baptist promotes an atmosphere of openness and love that encourages members to communicate their needs.

Generally speaking, all of First Baptist's ministries offered to persons outside the church are also made available to church members. Here are some specific ways the church tries to meet members' needs.

• When church members need money or shelter, these services are made available. At First Baptist the pastor uses discretionary funds to help members who find themselves in circumstances beyond their control. The use of these funds often opens the door to in-depth financial counseling that can help individuals gain better control of financial matters. In addition, financial workshops are offered to teach members to manage their money.

• The church addresses transportation needs by referring to mechanics persons whose cars need repair or maintenance.

• Home-care brigades of Christians skilled in home repair and maintenance are available to assist widows whose residences need repairs.

• The church's newsletter includes a needs-classified section, through which members make their needs known or convey their availability to help others.

• The church's Homebound Ministry reaches out with Jesus' love and hope to members who are sick at home or in nursing homes. The volunteers, trained to think of themselves as home missionaries, are assigned to five persons to whom they minister four times a year through personal visits, telephone calls, or cards. Each homebound person is assigned 13 missionaries so that the person receives ministry at least once every week and so that over the course of a year, the person receives visits from several missionaries. The missionaries minister in many ways, including Bible reading, prayer, encouragement, and acts of kindness. In several nursing homes in the Leesburg area, regular Bible studies are conducted for the residents. The ministry also extends to older adults who are hospitalized. Inevitably, the ministry also extends to their families, especially at times of illness or death. First Baptist's Homebound Ministry now includes 230 homebound adults and 250 who are in nursing facilities. Over 400 church members serve as missionaries to these persons. Not only has this ministry encouraged older adults who are Christians, but over the past four years more than 300 older adults have also accepted Christ as a result of the ministry.

Following are additional ways churches can meet needs in God's family.

Sunday School classes. Sunday School classes can be effective tools for delivering needed ministries to members with needs. Sunday School classes not only provide their members with Bible teaching that is essential to spiritual growth, but they also serve as the church's best link to its members and prospects. The small-group nature of most Sunday School classes provides a setting of intimacy and trust in which members' needs can be met. Often, the Sunday School teacher and the class members are the first in the church family to learn about a situation that calls for ministry, such as a death or an illness in a member's family, a divorce, or a job loss. The class is also usually the first to learn of good news that deserves a celebration. These facts put Sunday School classes in unique positions to minister to members of the body.

For this ministry to take place, Sunday School teachers, group leaders, and members need to be oriented toward ministry. A class must not become a clique, concerned about only a few persons or focused only on members' social needs. Rather, class members must be willing to reach out in loving actions and prayer. The class must give itself to service, especially to those experiencing difficulties or transitions. By doing so, a class can strongly support all of its members. In fact, it becomes the front line of ministry to members of the body of Christ.

Deacons. Deacons can become ministry partners with the pastor and the church staff in caring for church members' needs. The view of deacons as an administrative board that handles the church's business reflects a total misunderstanding of deacons' purpose. The word translated *deacon* is *diakonos,* which means *servant.* Churches generally choose the most respected church members to be deacons, and they trust what these persons do and say. However, God calls deacons not to be masters or bosses in the church but to serve the body of Christ. Most Bible students believe that the seven men selected by the early church were the first deacons or at least occupied the position of service that later became deacon. Remember that their job was to ensure that the needs of indigent widows were met (see Acts 6).

Deacons are at their best when ministering to the church family. Many churches assign every member to a deacon. This deacon keeps in touch with those assigned to him, providing whatever ministry might be needed. Recently, the deacons of the church I serve as pastor were assigned church members to whom they would minister. We all laughed when we realized that everyone was assigned to a deacon except the pastor and his wife. After the expected jokes that no deacon wanted to accept *that* responsibility, Larry, one of the deacons, volunteered to add us to his list. Since that time Larry has gone out of his way to let us know that he is available to us. Everyone needs the ministry of a deacon. Perhaps pastors and other staff ministers need it most of all.

Deacons are often faced with the need to minister to families in crisis. These deacons need ongoing training and practice in ministry to become competent and confident in their work. Many deacon groups study *Wise-*

Counsel: Skills for Lay Counseling. This LIFE₋ course is an invaluable help to deacons as they learn to minister to persons' needs. The most important necessity for deacons who wish to answer God's call to minister, however, is a genuine love for the Lord and His people. God will greatly use deacons who are motivated by love to keep the body of Christ in good health. Remember, only a healthy body can minister to broken persons.

Encouragers. The ministry of encouragers can make a difference in the lives of God's people. We meet Barnabas for the first time in Acts 4. We are told that he sold some property and presented the profits to the apostles to help meet believers' needs. This record of his generosity is worthy of notice, but something far more important is recorded. We are told that his given name was Joseph but that the apostles gave him the name Barnabas, "which means 'one who encourages' " (Acts 4:36, GNB). Interestingly, every subsequent mention of this man calls him *Barnabas.* Even more significantly, every time he is mentioned, he is always described as doing something to encourage someone. Encouragement was his gift, and Barnabas used it well.

Every congregation has "Barnabas members"—men, women, and youth who care enough to listen and encourage. They make life a little easier for everyone because they offer what most of us need more than anything else—someone to love and encourage us.

A woman in a Somerset, Kentucky, church is a Barnabas person. Her smile is beautiful, her enthusiasm contagious. Once when she was seeking God's will for her life, she asked God in prayer, "Lord, what do You want me to do?" She sensed God's answer: "I want you to love My people." At first she felt a little disappointment. Is this all God wanted of her—to love His people? But she decided if that was what God wanted, that was what she would do. Today her love and encouragement are evident everywhere in the church. Although she is a busy professional person, she gives much time and energy to encourage others, especially teenage girls.

The ministry of an encourager may not seem as specific or dramatic as other ministries. But no ministry is more important. Encouragers can help keep others from becoming discouraged and burned-out. Knowing that someone really cares can make a significant difference in someone's life. Barnabas was probably not as great a preacher or theologian as some of the early church leaders, but people knew that he cared. No doubt this is why he became a key worker in the gospel's expansion into the Gentile world (see Acts 11:19-26; 13:1-5). In the work of ministry evangelism today, the ministry of encouragement is essential to maintain the church's morale and spirit.

SERVING THE SERVERS

The ministries of First Baptist Church, Leesburg, require the work and sacrifice of hundreds of church members. Although the church has paid ministry directors, the work is largely done by laypersons. Pastor Charles Roesel raises a crucial question: Who serves the servers? This question is important in any church that attempts to minister. Those who give themselves to witnessing and helping the needy have their own needs that must be met if they are to have the spiritual, emotional, and physical strength to continue.

Evidence suggests that churches that expect more from their members usually experience growth. In addition, when members are challenged by worthy goals, they are likely to rise to those expectations. Still, a church must not take for granted those who minister to others. Rather, it should do whatever possible to support them in their work. At least three kinds of action are appropriate to serve those who serve.

Organization. It is important to provide a clearly focused, well-planned ministry in which persons can become involved. Often, Christians are challenged to witness and minister in such general terms that they cannot clearly identify what they are being called to do. A church that wants its members to minister should have clearly focused ministries in mind, not just ministry in general. For example, a pastor or a leader may urge members to minister to homebound and hospitalized older adults. Many who hear this plea will feel an inclination to perform this ministry; but unless a specific plan for ministering to this group is provided, very little sustained ministry is likely to take place. On the other hand, if a plan for ministry to older adults is in place, volunteers will likely respond with effective ministry.

The ministries of First Baptist Church, Leesburg, do not happen in a haphazard manner. When someone in the church feels that God has laid a ministry on his heart, an inquiry is made to determine whether a similar ministry already exists. If not, and if the ministry needs to be done, the interested person is directed to others who might be interested or perhaps to a ministry leader for specific help.

After appropriate preliminary steps are taken, a ministry manual must be developed, which serves as a guide to define the ministry and to state how the ministry is performed. First Baptist has developed manuals for all of the church's ministries. These vary according to the particular ministry, but each manual incorporates the following procedures for establishing a ministry.

1. Pray to God for guidance and leadership.

2. Form a committee to research, organize, and direct the ministry.
3. Complete a study or a community survey to document the need for the ministry.
4. Seek church support, including support from the pulpit; interest meetings, possibly with guest speakers; and a list of members who wish to become involved in the ministry.
5. Locate a facility or a meeting place for the ministry.
6. Prepare a budget for the ministry.
7. Determine available resources for the ministry.
8. Choose a director or a leader for the ministry.
9. Determine the rules and policies by which the ministry will operate.
10. Recruit volunteers for operating the ministry.
11. Order necessary supplies, such as Bibles, study materials, and tapes.
12. Set a time to begin the ministry.

Ministries are undertaken only when they have been clearly defined and carefully planned. Consequently, a person who is called to a particular ministry knows exactly what is required to be involved.

Training. Too often, Christians are asked to do work for which they are not trained. First Baptist, Leesburg, provides ongoing training for volunteers who serve in the ministries. Through this training the church attempts to accomplish the following goals.
1. Align spiritual gifts with service responsibility. The goal is for members to do what God has gifted them to do.
2. Provide training in relationships. This is essential for dealing with persons.
3. Develop the individual's devotional life and recognize Christ's lordship.
4. Provide work partners to share the load. This strategy helps workers avoid feelings of isolation and promotes a team or family spirit.
5. Offer training in the area of service, which may involve LIFE® courses, support groups, seminars, books, and workshops.
6. Plan times for sharing and debriefing with others involved in ministry.

Almost everyone involved in ministry at First Baptist is expected to take the LIFE® course *WiseCounsel: Skills for Lay Counseling,* a study that equips volunteers with valuable listening-and-ministry skills. Other ministry training was described earlier in this chapter as a part of discipleship training.

Service groups. Further support for servers at First Baptist is provided through service groups. Basically, these groups are composed of those who work in a particular area of ministry. Their purpose is to provide a trusting atmosphere in which volunteers within a particular ministry can express their needs, pray for one another, and often have their needs met. In reality, these are support groups that help workers not to become discouraged or burned-out in their ministries. For example, those who work in the church's benevolence ministry constantly encounter needy persons' social, emotional, and physical stress. The service group gives these dedicated workers the opportunity to share frustrations and feelings related to the ministry. Group members can also work together to plan ways to carry on the work more effectively.

Within these service groups genuine *koinonia* takes place. The closeness that develops in the service groups is essential to the ongoing work of ministry and witness. Through this process ministry workers are strengthened and become more effective in their ministries.

This chapter has focused on the church's health and fitness as the body of Christ in the world. Only a healthy body can minister effectively. The church must not become so concerned about itself that it fails to hear a lost world's cries for help, but neither can the church attempt to respond to those cries without maintaining emotional and spiritual health.

The most important ingredient God can use in a church to heal this broken world is love—God's love for His people, our love for Him that inspires us to serve, and our love for one another that causes us to support fellow believers in unity and to share with the lost and hurting. John Drakeford tells an imagined but probable story about the apostle John, who was transformed by Christ's power from a fiery son of thunder to a man who was best known for his love. As an old man, feeble with age, he was carried to the gatherings of Christians. Rather than delivering a sermon, he would simply say, "Little children, love one another." When some grew tired of hearing this same admonition many times, one elder asked, "Master, why dost thou always say this?"

The aged apostle replied, "It is the Lord's command, and if this alone is done, it is enough."[7]

For any church that wants to win persons to Christ by touching them in their pain and sin, love is still the key.

---

[1] All resources mentioned by title in this chapter are available from the Customer Service Center; 127 Ninth Avenue, North; Nashville, TN 37234; 1-800-458-2772; and from Baptist Book Stores and Lifeway Christian Stores. For more information on products, write to Adult Discipleship and Family Department, MSN 151; the Sunday School Board; 127 Ninth Avenue, North; Nashville, TN 37234.

[2] Ken Hemphill, *The Official Rule Book for the New Church Game* (Nashville: Broadman Press, 1990), 106.

[3]Bobby L. Eklund, *Partners with God: Bible Truths About Giving* (Nashville: Convention Press, 1994), 6.

[4]Johnny Jones, comp., *LIFE® Support Leader's Handbook* (Nashville: LifeWay Press, 1993), 8–9.

[5]Ibid., 9.

[6]Ibid., 12.

[7]John W. Drakeford, *This Insanity Called Love* (Waco: Word, 1970), 150.

Getting on God's Agenda

IMAGINE YOURSELF in a meeting your manager has called. When you walk into the conference room at 8:00 a.m., you find that the other four persons scheduled to attend are already seated around the conference table. Joe and Zachary are drinking coffee and discussing the meeting they will conduct next week in another state. Lisa, to be married in three months, expresses her hope that this meeting will not make her late for her lunch date with her fiancé. Larry, your manager, sits at the end of the table, looking through the sales reports he has just received. You are thankful that the wreck on the interstate did not make you late for the meeting but are anxious about changes in the company's health-care plan that were recently announced.

As the meeting begins, Larry announces that the sales report issued this morning indicates a serious decline in sales. He states that the group must spend the day determining how to address this problem. Lunch will be brought in to make best use of the available time, and all out-of-town meetings for the next 30 days will be postponed. Only the problem of declining sales will be the focus for the immediate future.

Obviously, participants had a variety of agendas in mind when this meeting began, but Larry changed that. This meeting would address only one agenda. The same situation can exist in a church. Often, mixed or conflicting agendas are represented.

- The pastor may believe that constructing a new building or increasing the budget offerings is the most necessary priority for the church.
- The deacons may believe that the present facilities are adequate and that increased pastoral visitation and care are more important than a new building.
- Others may believe that a strong youth program is the church's greatest need.
- Others may feel that the church must give primary attention to marriage, parenting, and family issues.
- Still others may consider missions the church's main agenda, reminding

members that millions have never heard the gospel.

• Some members may be overwhelmed by the community's tremendous social needs. Persons are homeless, hungry, and cold. Children are deprived of medical care. The elderly are reduced to poverty. These members argue that the church's function is to relieve human suffering through social ministry.

Most agendas expressed by church leaders and members are worthy ones. Nevertheless, a church can fall victim to agenda fragmentation when it follows so many agendas that every ministry or program suffers. Every church needs a unifying purpose, a rationale for all the church does, whether it involves worship, music, youth, pastoral ministries, building programs, budgets, missions, or social ministry. In the midst of the many agendas about what the church should be and do, the question must be asked, What is God's agenda for the church? Ministry evangelism, at its very heart, means getting on God's agenda.

JESUS' AGENDA

The disciples had gone into a Samaritan village to buy food as Jesus rested by a well in Samaria (see John 4:6-8). There Jesus had an encounter with a Samaritan woman whom we call the woman at the well. The story is well known. The woman had a confused and sordid past. As Jesus talked with her, she grew to understand her need for something that could bring lasting peace to her troubled life (see John 4:7-26). Thrilled with her newfound hope and forgiveness, the woman ran into the village to tell everyone (see John 4:28-30).

When the disciples returned, they offered food to Jesus but were bewildered by His response: " 'I have food to eat that you know nothing about' " (John 4:32). When they questioned Him, He responded, " 'My food is to do the will of him who sent me and to finish his work' " (John 4:34). These powerful words define Jesus' agenda: to do the Father's will by finishing the work He was sent to do. What was that work? It was the work of redeeming persons—like the woman whom He had just given a new reason for living. As Jesus thought of persons' needs like those of the Samaritan woman's, He said: " 'I tell you, open your eyes and look at the fields! They are ripe for harvest' " (John 4:35). To Jesus, the harvest was persons. Persons were His agenda.

Leonard Griffith writes about the account of Jesus and the demon-possessed man who lived among the tombs. As Jesus set the man free from the powers that bound him, He permitted the demons to go into a herd of swine nearby. The possessed man was made whole (see Mark 5:15). However, those who lost the pigs were not pleased. As a result, they "began to plead with Jesus to leave their region" (Mark 5:17). The people were really saying: "You care for men; we care for swine. That's where we differ, so get out!"[1] Griffith summarizes: "The farmers put pigs first, people second. Jesus put people first, pigs second. People were his priority."[2] Again we see that persons—even persons like that demon-possessed man—were Jesus' agenda.

Our agendas grow from our priorities. We carry out our daily work on the basis of what we believe is most important. Every person has priorities. Leonard Griffith states that a person's priorities can be revealed by the answers to three questions: (1) What does the person have time for? (2) How does the person spend his wealth? (3) What does the person allow to interrupt him? By applying these questions to Jesus, Griffith says, we can understand what His priorities were during His earthly ministry.

What did Jesus have time for? He was incredibly busy. Sometimes He did not have time to eat or sleep. He had to train His disciples, teach the truths of the Kingdom, and deal with the mounting opposition of the religious authorities. He knew that time was running out; yet He always took time for persons. He even had time for children who were brought to Him (see Mark 10:14-16).

How did Jesus spend His wealth? He had no money or earthly wealth, but He had far greater wealth in God's power. He could have used this tremendous power for Himself, but He always used it to minister to persons' needs. The Gospel accounts of Jesus' many healing miracles testify to the way He used His power. A dramatic example of Jesus' use of His power was His assuming the role of a servant to wash His disciples' feet (see John 13:3-5). Rather than use His power for His own needs, Jesus served His disciples in a memorable way. Jesus spent His wealth on persons.

What did Jesus allow to interrupt Him? Jesus allowed persons to interrupt Him. Griffith writes: "It didn't matter what he was doing—preaching a sermon, eating a meal, taking his rest, praying—he could always be interrupted by persons who needed him. Persons were his priority. He put persons first."[3]

Because persons were Jesus' priority, persons became His agenda. Everything He lived, said, and did reflects this agenda. He lived for persons, gave Himself without reserve for persons, and finally died for persons.

Jesus' concern for persons touched every area of their lives. The Gospels are filled with accounts of Jesus' healing and helping persons, but we must not imagine that His concern was purely for the physical. Jesus was concerned for whole persons—body, mind, and spirit. He definitely gave priority to persons' spiritual needs. On one occasion Jesus was teaching in a crowded house in Capernaum. So many had gathered to hear Him teach that no room was left even to crowd inside the door. Four men attempted to bring their afflicted friend to Jesus on a mat. When they could not enter the house because of the crowd, they climbed onto the roof, cut a hole in it, and lowered their friend into the room where Jesus was teaching. Jesus was amazed at the faith of these four men. Before the encounter ended, the sick man was healed and was able to walk home.

Significantly, Jesus did not start with the man's physical needs when He ministered to him. The man definitely had serious physical problems. Jesus was concerned about these needs and ministered to them. But because Jesus' first priority was the man's spiritual need, His first words to him were " 'Son, your sins are forgiven' " (Mark 2:5). Before He healed the man's broken body, He healed him spiritually. Jesus ministered to the whole person. He did not minimize the physical need, but He always gave priority to the spiritual need. He knew far better than we that the physical is temporal, while the spiritual relates to eternity.

Jesus' agenda was always redemptive. When He fed the hungry, healed the sick, lifted the fallen, and strengthened the weak, His ministry always extended beyond the physical. Jesus always reached into the person's heart and sought to bring that individual into a saving relationship with the Father. He plainly expressed His agenda, the redemption of the whole person, when He said, " 'The Son of Man came to seek and to save what was lost' " (Luke 19:10).

STICKING TO THE MAIN AGENDA

Sometimes evangelical believers regard helping ministries with suspicion, protesting that persons' spiritual needs are far greater than the need for food, shelter, and other material goods. Without Christ, persons are lost; and no amount of social action can meet that need. Often, we hear the social gospel negatively referred to as no gospel at all, since it does not speak to the most serious human needs—lostness and condemnation.

Much of this opinion springs from legitimate concerns about faulty theology. The religious and educational world has been affected by powerful figures in the early 20th century, such as Frederick R. Tennant and John Dewey. Basically, these and other thinkers advanced an unbiblical view of human nature that rejected the idea of original sin. In this way of thinking, persons are seen as basically good. The concept of sin is scarcely mentioned. A logical outcome of this thinking is the belief that persons belong to God's kingdom because they are essentially good. According to this optimistic view of humanity, persons have no need for personal salvation. To such thinkers, humans' main problem is not sin but ignorance. If persons can overcome that ignorance and can recognize their essential goodness, all will be well.[4]

From this erroneous theology grew the utopian idea that if persons' ignorance can be overcome and their living conditions improved, they can achieve their place as God's children. This philosophy even gave rise to churches that practiced social ministries without addressing the spiritual need for forgiveness of sin and reconciliation with God.

Although this theology may sound appealing, it is false. We are sinners. Our nature is predisposed toward sin, and only Jesus Christ's redeeming power can set us free and redeem us. The Bible makes very clear that people—all people—are sinners (see Rom. 3:23). Findley B. Edge writes that all of humanity, not just part, is infected by sin. This does not mean that individuals are incapable of doing good things but that "every thought and act is contaminated by the fact of sin."[5] Second, Edge reminds us that the question is not just one of individual sinfulness. Rather, "sin is the characteristic of the whole human race." Edge speaks of this as "the solidarity of sin." Everyone is involved in this sinful situation, including all human structures and organizations.[6] Third, Edge writes of sin's inevitability. Every person is a sinner by nature and by choice. Although each person is part of the sinful situation posed by original sin, every person is responsible for his own sin. Sin, says Edge, is "a personal and responsible act. It is a personal revolt against God, which is aggravated by society and its shortcomings but which is nevertheless our personal responsibility."[7] Edge concludes: "Man is a sinner! ... No philosophy of religious education and no program of the church can be adequate that does not place this fundamental fact at its center."[8]

Understandably, evangelicals would look with suspicion on social action without evangelism. Social action alone does not meet a person's deepest needs. Christians should support and participate in community efforts to meet needs and to confront problems like hunger and homelessness. But the church's business goes deeper. As Christians, we are to feed the hungry, shelter the homeless, and protect the innocent to express God's love to persons so that they will come to know Him as Savior and Lord. Our caring ministry must be unconditional, but it must always carry the gospel message.

The apostle Paul addressed our ministry responsibility in these words: "All this is from God, who reconciled us to himself through Christ and gave us the ministry of reconciliation" (2 Cor. 5:18). Those of us who have been reconciled to God (saved) have been given a ministry. This ministry is the ministry of reconciliation. The question is, What does it mean to be a minister of reconciliation?

Findley B. Edge points out that many Christians have related reconciliation only to saving souls; therefore, the one focus of the Christian's ministry is evangelism, or soul-winning. This view, according to Edge, adopts the Greek dualistic view of human life that sees a person as a body and a soul. This view tends to emphasize the importance of the spiritual and to give little attention to the physical. A more biblical view sees a person as a unit and is concerned with the physical, emotional, social, and spiritual aspects of life. God is concerned with the totality of a person's life; therefore, reconciliation involves the total person and all of his relationships and circumstances.[9] William Pinson speaks about the need to include the whole person in our ministry efforts: "Not only are we to minister to all persons but we are to minister to all needs. Jesus fixed his ministry on whole people, not on bodies as some medical technicians might, nor on minds as some educators do, nor on emotions as some counselors and psychiatrists do, nor on souls as some religionists do. He was concerned about whole people."[10] Reconciliation brings persons into relationship with God by ministering to every area of their lives.

Part of our role in bringing God's redemptive love to others is influencing the structures of society that are detrimental to humanity's well-being. Christians must work to make conditions better for others, especially the downtrodden and powerless. We can do so by becoming involved in both Christian social action and Christian social ministry. Christian social ministry refers to deeds of love and kindness that meet individual needs, such as feeding the hungry, clothing the ragged, and ministering to the sick and imprisoned. On the other hand, Christian social action refers to the efforts of God's people to make needed changes in society to alleviate conditions that hurt others, especially the poor and underclassed.[11] Christians must not only minister to persons' hurt and brokenness but also try to eliminate the evils in society that create pain, poverty, and suffering.

Delos Miles uses the story of the good Samaritan in Luke 10:25-37 to illustrate the difference between Christian social ministry and Christian social action. The Samaritan engaged in social ministry by binding the beaten man's wounds and by spending time and money to save his life. "If he had sought to change the conditions which led to the Jericho road robbery and mugging, that would have been social action."[12]

Many believers and churches were involved in social action in the 1960s and 1970s to bring racial justice to a segregated nation. In this decade Christians take stands on societal issues such as abortion, legalized gambling, crime, and drug trafficking. More attention needs to be given to social justice in areas such as housing, nutrition, and medical care.

Christians should be passionate about the causes they believe in; but the church's witness is negated when Christians become shrill, hateful, and violent. Christians must not let themselves be led to extremism, hatred, and violence. As we attack society's injustices that damage persons, we must do so in the spirit of our Lord—the spirit of redemptive love.

Our agenda, like that of Jesus, is to do God's work in the world. This means involvement in caring for persons' needs and hurts in order to introduce them to Jesus, the Great Physician.

WHAT IS MINISTRY?

A church in Virginia has a unique sign in front of the church building. Beneath the name of the church and the schedule of weekly services is the word *Ministers*. A passerby would expect to find listed the names of the pastor, the minister of music, the minister of education, and perhaps other staff ministers; but this is not the case. Instead, beneath the word *Ministers* are these words: *All 650 members of the church*. Although this may be unusual, it is biblically accurate. Every Christian is a minister.

Affirming the ministry responsibilities of all believers does not diminish the roles of pastors and other leaders. God calls certain individuals to specific areas of ministry. We must never lose sight of the fact that God's call to these areas is real and that these roles are absolutely essential. Before considering all believers' ministry responsibilities, let's identify the roles of those who are called to what we refer to as full-time Christian service. Look at the key New Testament passage that speaks to this matter: "It was he who gave some to be apostles, some to be prophets, some to be evangelists, and some to be pastors and teachers, to prepare God's people for works of service, so that the body of Christ may be built up" (Eph. 4:11-12). God gives the especially gifted and divinely called leaders to the church to prepare His people for service and ministry. The word translated *prepare* in Ephesians 4:12 is *katartismos*. This word can refer to mending a fisher's nets so that he is prepared for fishing. Leaders mend, equip, and prepare God's people for ministry.[13] The role of pastors and other leaders is not to perform all the church's ministry while the church members pray for them, encourage them, and give money to make it possible. Instead, the role of called leaders is to provide the training, encouragement, and opportunity for every church member to be a minister in God's church and in His world.

The division often made between clergy and laity is artificial, causing persons to believe that ordinary believers are spectators and supporters or critics of those who perform ministry. This false clergy-laity dualism has led to the heretical idea that the word *laity* is synonymous with *amateur,* while church leaders at the staff level are considered professionals. "The result has been a loss of identity by the laity; and the clergy has become so over-burdened by the enormity of its task that no one seems happy—clergyman or layman alike."[14]

God never intended for the pastor and other staff members to do all the church's ministry. Christians cannot pay anyone to do the ministry God expects them to perform. Every Christian is called to ministry. This is not negotiable. The only question is whether a believer will accept the responsibility or reject it.

Sometimes it is said that for a Christian everything is ministry. Although this might be true in a general sense, the statement is dangerous. Every Christian is a minister. Therefore, we represent Christ in every relationship, business dealing, and word spoken. But living the Christian life or performing isolated instances of kindness or witness is not intentional ministry. In other words, Christians do not do ministry by just living the Christian life, going to church faithfully, or doing the things Christians are ordinarily expected to do.

In describing the type of ministry Christians are called to perform in the world, Findley B. Edge adds the adjective *focused* to the word *ministry* to distinguish it from the ordinary, daily things all Christians are supposed to do. Then he suggests six ingredients of focused ministry that are necessary for Christians to get on God's agenda:

1. Focused ministry is *specific.* "It is specific in the sense that one can state what it is with clarity and can state clearly how this ministry is expressed." This characteristic helps us avoid the problem of vagueness.
2. Focused ministry has *significance.* "That is, it must be something that has significance and worth in terms of human need and God's redemptive purpose." Edge also insists that ministry must be significant in proportion to the time and effort it demands.
3. Focused ministry must be something to which a person is *called by God.* God calls all Christians to love Him and serve Him, but He also calls us to specific ministry. Discerning God's will is a matter each believer must deal with, but a clear sense of God's call is vital to ministry.
4. Focused ministry is *consciously chosen.* The person chooses the ministry from a desire to respond to God's call. Edge warns: "It is not something one does because one has had a 'guilt trip' laid on him or her. Rather it is a ministry to which one commits oneself with utmost seriousness."
5. Focused ministry is one for which God has given the person *gifts* to ful-

fill. The church should recognize and affirm these gifts.

6. Focused ministry must support *God's redemptive purpose*. As Edge puts it, "This ministry should be directly involved in fulfilling God's redemptive purpose in the world. That is leading people to know Jesus as Savior and Lord in their personal lives and ministering to the human brokenness in the lives of people and society."[15]

In clarifying the difference between ministry and daily Christian living, these ingredients of focused ministry can help Christians be specific in identifying the ministries to which God has called them.

DOES EVERY CHRISTIAN HAVE A GIFT FOR MINISTRY?

We have seen that church leaders are called to prepare believers for service and ministry. Darrell W. Robinson writes: "The biblical principle of equipping the people of God is the hope of the church. It is the church's hope for being built up within by the dynamic of the Christ-life. It is the church's hope for fulfillment of the mission of Jesus in the world."[16] Equipping God's people for ministry evangelism must include helping them discover and use their spiritual gifts. Gift discovery, development, and use are key ways for Christians to get on God's agenda for ministry and to be equipped for the task.

What are spiritual gifts? Who has them? What is their purpose? How can individual Christians discover their spiritual gifts? What happens when believers discover and use spiritual gifts?

Tragically, most Christians do not understand spiritual gifts and do not imagine that they have one or more spiritual gifts. Many assume that spiritual gifts are not for all Christians but only for the elite few. Some even have the idea that if a person has a gift of the Spirit, it will be expressed in a spectacular, dramatic, or even bizarre way. Some Christians might even feel that those who talk about spiritual gifts are fanatics, best left to their own strange ideas. Perhaps, some would say, it is best not to deal with something we do not understand. For such persons the less said about the subject, the better. After all, we do not want persons to become religious fanatics. These views are tragic misunderstandings because God carries out the work of His body, the church, through the use of spiritual gifts. In fact, "a church becomes a body when it is 'gifted' by the Holy Spirit."[17]

Four New Testament passages deal specifically with the gifts of the Spirit. The gifts listed in these passages are shown on the chart on the following page.

Romans 12:6-8	1 Corinthians 12:28
1. Prophesying	1. Apostles
2. Serving	2. Prophets
3. Teaching	3. Teachers
4. Encouraging	4. Workers of miracles
5. Contributing to the needs of others	5. Healing
6. Leadership	6. Ability to help others
7. Showing mercy	7. Administration
	8. Speaking in different kinds of tongues

1 Corinthians 12:8-10
1. Message of wisdom
2. Message of knowledge
3. Faith
4. Healing
5. Miraculous powers
6. Prophecy
7. Distinguishing between spirits
8. Speaking in different kinds of tongues
9. The interpretation of tongues

Ephesians 4:11
1. Apostles
2. Prophets
3. Evangelists
4. Pastors
5. Teachers

A casual examination of these lists reveals that some gifts are identified with specific persons, such as pastors, apostles, evangelists, prophets, and teachers. These gifted individuals are God's gift to the church. Remember, these leaders' purpose is "to prepare God's people for works of service" (Eph. 4:12). These individuals are gifted to equip Christians to minister as God's people in the world. If these leaders simply become great orators and teachers without performing their equipping function, they miss the main purpose of their calling. If they do the church's work while the members serve as spectators or cheerleaders, they deprive the church of its opportunity to be the ministering body of Christ in the community and the world.

The remaining gifts relate to ministry functions, such as showing mercy, healing, giving, and leading. Members of the body of Christ have been given these gifts to carry on the church's ministries. If leaders such as pastors and teachers help believers discover, develop, and use their gifts, the local body of Christ will minister with power and effectiveness that result not from human resources and personalities but from God's power.

"When the spiritual gifts are operating in a congregation to equip it for various Christian ministries, it is the mighty God who is at work."[18]

When the four lists of spiritual gifts are compared and combined, 18 distinct gifts are identified. One resource places the gifts in four categories:

Gifts of Serving	**Gifts of Worshiping**
1. Helps	1. Prophecy
2. Mercy	2. Spiritual discernment
3. Giving	3. Exhortation (encouragement)
4. Healing	4. Shepherding (pastoring)
Gifts of Teaching	**Gifts of Witnessing**
1. Wisdom	1. Faith
2. Knowledge	2. Evangelism
3. Teaching	3. Apostleship
4. Leadership (administration)	4. Miracles[19]

This list does not include the gifts of speaking in tongues and the interpretation of tongues. These gifts would best fit the category of worshiping.

It is not necessary to force the gifts into categories because the gifts listed in the Scriptures are representative, not exhaustive. Some of the gifts listed may no longer be operative in the church, at least not in the same way they were originally. For example, the Corinthian church gave great importance to the gifts of tongues and the interpretation of tongues; but those gifts are not mentioned in the Romans list. Although some believers have attached great importance to these gifts in our day, most Bible students see little use for those gifts. On the other hand, such gifts as mercy, encouragement, teaching, and evangelism have relevance to the church in every age. Ken Hemphill writes: "These lists are representative, not exhaustive. They were intended only to illustrate the sort of abilities and activities one might call 'spiritual gifts.' There is no value in combining the various lists and identifying twelve or sixteen gifts. God is a God of infinite creativity, and He is still creating gifts for the church today as it faces new challenges and tasks."[20]

Lewis Drummond recalls a lecture by John Stott suggesting the probable existence of thousands of spiritual gifts. Drummond adds: "Every age, culture, generation, and situation has its specific needs. Surely the Spirit will step into these needs and 'gift' His people to meet them."[21] God gifts

His people with whatever they need to do His work in the world. This is as certain in our day as it was when Paul spoke of spiritual gifts two thousand years ago.

Ken Hemphill warns of two dangers in regard to spiritual gifts. One is overemphasis. When Christians make so much of their gifts that they become overly proud of them, they can become spiritually arrogant and elitist. Apparently, spiritual gifts had become a matter of pride in the church at Corinth. The second danger in regard to spiritual gifts is underemphasis. Some Christians do not believe that they have spiritual gifts and therefore feel that they can do nothing in the church's ministry. Hemphill concludes, "Any Christian who fails to utilize his or her gift in service to the church deprives the body of Christ and is guilty of bad stewardship."[22]

The subject of spiritual gifts always raises questions. Biblical answers are important because unless believers discover, develop, and use their gifts, they will not be effective ministers of the Lord Jesus Christ. The following are some of the most frequently asked questions about spiritual gifts.

Where do spiritual gifts come from? This question is easy to answer. Spiritual gifts come only from God the Holy Spirit. Apparently, the believers in the church at Corinth wrote to Paul to ask a series of questions, and Paul responded in what we call 1 Corinthians. One question must have related to the gifts of the Spirit, because Paul began what we know as chapter 12 with these words: "Now about spiritual gifts, brothers" (v. 1). In the remainder of the chapter Paul addressed spiritual gifts and their relationship to the body of Christ. In verse 4 Paul wrote, "There are different kinds of gifts, but the same Spirit." In verse 6 he wrote, "There are different kinds of working, but the same God works all of them in all men." Then he included the brief phrases "through the Spirit," "by means of the same Spirit," "by that one Spirit" as he listed the gifts (see vv. 8-10). He summed up the subject in verse 11: "All these are the work of one and the same Spirit." Spiritual gifts are supernatural gifts, given by the Spirit.

Are spiritual gifts the same as talents? The answer to that question is no! Many persons—Christians and non-Christians—have wonderful talents that can be used to contribute to humanity's well-being and enrichment. For example, a great composer or artist can produce works of beauty and art that improve life for all of us. Although talents are God-given, they are not the same as spiritual gifts. Spiritual gifts are given only to believers by the Holy Spirit to equip them for God's work in the church and in the world.

Spiritual gifts and talents may blend. A strong relationship may exist between a person's natural talents and spiritual gifts. God often gives a person natural talent, then, when that person becomes a Christian, gives spiritual gifts that utilize those talents. God is sovereign. He is the giver of talents and spiritual gifts.

How many spiritual gifts exist? Most Bible students agree that the gifts listed in Scripture are not meant to be seen as final or exhaustive. Paul did not list the same gifts in each instance. Apparently, different gifts were given at different times and in different places. The same is true in the church today. God gives what is needed in each expression of His body. Probably, hundreds, even thousands, of spiritual gifts exist.

What is the purpose of spiritual gifts? The Corinthian church was a troubled church. Many problems and controversies were tearing the church apart. In the Corinthian letters Paul dealt with many of these problems. One problem he addressed in 1 Corinthians was spiritual gifts. First Corinthians 14, for example, addresses the matter of *glossolalia,* or speaking in tongues. Apparently, some believers in Corinth had exalted and misused this relatively minor gift to the point that Paul found it necessary to give careful instructions for using the gift (see 1 Cor. 14:9-25,39-40). *Glossolalia* had probably become a matter of spiritual pride in the Corinthian church, with the tongues speakers regarded as spiritually elite. Perhaps it had become such a symbol of spirituality that those who could not claim the gift were considered inferior Christians.

Paul reminded the Corinthians that the purpose of spiritual gifts is to equip each church member to function in the body of Christ (see 1 Cor. 12:12-31). The gifts' purpose is simply stated in 1 Corinthians 12:7: "Now to each one the manifestation of the Spirit is given for the common good." Clearly, spiritual gifts are given for the benefit of the entire body. Through the use of spiritual gifts, the body of Christ can minister in the world. Spiritual gifts are not given so that Christians can lift themselves up with pride, nor are they given to make us happy. Spiritual gifts are given to equip us to serve as part of the body of Christ.

Spiritual gifts are really grace gifts. When Paul introduced the subject of spiritual gifts in his letter to the Corinthians, he used the word *pneumatika,* or *spiritual gifts.* Apparently, this was the word the Corinthians used when they raised the question. But when Paul began to respond to their questions, he used another word, *charismata,* which is best translated *grace gifts.* Spiritual gifts are really gifts of God's grace. Our gracious God has given us the gifts to enable us to serve Him and the people He loves.

Who has spiritual gifts? Are spiritual gifts given only to certain Christians? The view that only "professionals" are gifted for ministry, while "ordinary" Christians have a supportive role, is unbiblical and destructive to the church's ministry. Paul wrote, "Now to each one the manifestation of the Spirit is given" (1 Cor. 12:7). Then, speaking of gifts, he wrote, "All these are the work of one and the same Spirit, and he gives them to each one, just as he determines" (1 Cor. 12:11). The phrase "each one" indicates that each member of the Corinthian church had one or more spiritual gifts. Many believers have not yet discovered their gifts or used them, but every Christian has one or more gifts.

Why do different spiritual gifts exist? Paul wrote to the Roman church, "We have different gifts, according to the grace given us" (Rom. 12:6). Christians have different gifts for the same reason the human body has hands, eyes, ears, and feet. It is a matter of function. Paul put it this way: "Just as each of us has one body with many members, and these members do not all have the same function, so in Christ we who are many form one body, and each member belongs to all the others" (Rom. 12:4-5). As with the human body, diversity is important in the body of Christ because each member has a vital function to perform. The church is truly healthy only when all members work as they are designed to work. All parts are different, but they all work together.

We are called not to be carbon copies of one another but to discover our unique gifts and to exercise them. When all of the different gifts are being used, the church, the body of Christ, functions the way God intends. When individual members do not discover and use their spiritual gifts, the church does not function as God intends. A church that does not help members identify and use their gifts is dysfunctional; it simply does not work properly.

Many times, church members are made to feel guilty for not doing tasks for which they have no gifts. For example, persons who do not have the gift of teaching may be persuaded to teach a Sunday School class. The result is discouragement, burnout, and poor teaching. Too many churches pursue the goal of merely filling positions. The biblical approach is to help believers discover and develop their gifts, then to place them where they are gifted to serve. This principle applies to every area of God's work. All Christians are called to witness, but not all have the gift of evangelism. All Christians are called to care about others; but not all have the gift of mercy, which would qualify them to work in a rescue mission or in a ministry to abused women.

Christians should not feel inferior or guilty because they cannot do what other Christians can do. Many different gifts exist. In fact, all of the gifts a church needs to function as a complete body are present in every church, large or small. This is why it is so important that church leaders help believers discover, develop, and use their gifts (see Eph. 4:11-12). All of the available gifts need to be revealed and utilized for a church to carry out the ministries God intends for it to do.

How can spiritual gifts be discovered? Spiritual gifts are not intended to be just another topic of study and discussion. They must be discovered, developed, and used if they are to benefit the body of Christ. No doubt many churches operate at half their capacity because the members have been neither guided to discover their gifts nor permitted to use them in ministry. Ministry evangelism especially depends on the discovery and use of spiritual gifts because it cannot be done by the pastor and staff alone, even if unlimited funding were provided for the ministries. Ministry evangelism requires that large numbers of members minister by using their spiritual gifts.

Often, ministry evangelism is born from the pastor's vision and conviction, as with First Baptist Church of Leesburg, Florida. Pastor Charles Roesel has a heart for persons and compassion for their hurts and needs. He has taught members the biblical truths that undergird ministry evangelism and has sought to be an example of caring to his congregation. But First Baptist's more than 70 ministries are not Charles Roesel's ministries. Nor do they belong to the ministry directors who have been employed as the ministries have rapidly grown. Ministry evangelism at First Baptist requires the involvement of hundreds of church members. Answering God's call to minister, these Christians began by discovering their spiritual gifts. Gift discovery is vital to a congregation's ongoing ministry.

The following suggestions can facilitate the process by which church members discover and use their spiritual gifts.

Leaders must be willing to help Christians discover and use their spiritual gifts. Pastors and other ministers cannot do all the church's ministry while members watch, support, and applaud. They must help members understand that they are gifted and called for ministry. This can be done through the ongoing practice of preaching, teaching, affirming, equipping, and enabling members to discover and use their spiritual gifts.

A pastor or another leader must be willing to trust the Holy Spirit's leadership in this area. If church leaders feel that they must control everything in the church's ministry, they are unlikely to permit members to use their gifts. Pastors must lead their people wisely, but God is sovereign. He gives gifts to His people "just as he determines" (1 Cor. 12:11). The gifts are His to give. The church is His to control. Leaders must not be afraid to encourage gift discovery. Pastors are "player coaches." They develop and use the gifts God has given them for ministry; they also affirm, train, and enable members to use their gifts in ministry. Members are not likely to discover their gifts unless church leaders encourage them to do so.

Christians must want to discover their spiritual gifts. Paul encouraged the Corinthian Christians to "eagerly desire the greater gifts" (1 Cor. 12:31). Every believer has one or more spiritual gifts. Sadly, many Christians do not know that they are gifted for ministry. Even more sadly, some Christians are not interested in discovering their gifts. An individual must be open to the Holy Spirit in order to discover his gifts.

God has many ways of revealing spiritual gifts to His people. God speaks through His Word, through prayer, through open doors of opportunity, and through others' influence. But believers must hunger to hear His voice through these means. God is less likely to speak to a person about spiritual gifts if that person is complacent and unconcerned about spiritual truth.

In addition, God will not reveal our gifts to us if our motivation for this knowledge is purely self-centered. Spiritual gifts are given not to make us look or feel good but to equip the body of Christ to function effectively. Spiritual gifts are given "for the common good" (1 Cor. 12:7). As we seek to discover our gifts, our motivation must be ministry for God's glory.

Christians should consider their natural talents and growing interests. We learned earlier that talents and spiritual gifts are not the same; everyone has talents, while only Christians have spiritual gifts. However, a Christian's talents and spiritual gifts are often closely related. God can give a believer a gift that is unique or new, but usually this is not the case. When we trust the Lord Jesus for salvation, God gives the Holy Spirit to us. The indwelling Spirit then makes it possible for us to understand spiritual truth (see 1 Cor. 2:9-12). Because the Spirit lives in us, we are able to look at our natural talents in a new way as gifts from our gracious God. Often, these abilities are elevated by the Spirit and become His gifts to the body. As Ken Hemphill writes, "Rather than receiving new abilities not previously possessed, often new believers begin to see their abilities in a new light."[23]

Spiritual gifts can also be discovered by paying attention to developing interests. God speaks in different ways to different persons. To some, the discovery of a gift may come dramatically and suddenly. However, the Holy Spirit is more likely to work quietly over a period of time to create an interest in an area of ministry and service.

Sandy Jones was a secretary at First Baptist Church in Leesburg, Florida. One Sunday morning in 1989 Pastor Roesel preached a sermon with the title "Satan's Contract on Our Children." Sandy's heart was stirred. Although she taught a Sunday School class for four-year-olds, she did not feel that she was making a significant difference in the children's lives and began to feel restlessness in her spirit. When the director of the Children's Shelter asked Sandy if she would occasionally take a child home with her for an evening, she eagerly agreed. The children began to tug at Sandy's heart, and she began to experience overwhelming joy that her family could share time with them.

Sandy started working as a volunteer at the Children's Shelter. Soon she was asked to be the director of the church's Latchkey Ministry, but she did not feel that the timing was right to say yes. Later, in a study of *Experiencing God: Knowing and Doing the Will of God* Sandy learned how to watch and listen for God's leadership, to find where He is at work, and to join Him in that work. Once again she was approached about the Latchkey Ministry. This time Sandy fasted and prayed to discover God's will. She asked God to affirm His will by leading the pastor to be positive about her leaving the church office and accepting the position. When Pastor Roesel gave his support and encouragement, Sandy had her answer.

Since Sandy became the director of this ministry, God has used her gifts to minister to many families. Numerous family members have come to Christ through the Latchkey Ministry.

God often leads us one step at a time to realize that our talents and emerging interests are His way to help us discover our spiritual gifts. Christians should consider their talents and interests viable avenues for discovering the ministry gifts God has given them.

An inventory can help Christians discover their spiritual gifts. An instrument like the one in appendix 1 can be used to reveal spiritual gifts. To complete the inventory, believers express feelings and preferences about different expressions of ministry. Then they score the inventory to determine the degree to which various gifts are present in their lives.

Several years ago I was leading a study of spiritual gifts at a retreat. When the group completed the inventory, I did so too. I was baffled when my inventory indicated that I have the gift of healing. When I thought of the gift of healing, I thought of someone in biblical times who laid hands on the physically sick to mediate God's healing to them. I knew that I did not have this ability. As I prayed about what I had discovered, God seemed to say: "Healing is not limited to physical needs. Many persons have emotional, relational, and spiritual needs." I realized that God had gifted me to help individuals and churches find reconciliation. As I recalled the churches I had served as the pastor, I realized that my role had usually been that of a healer. No, I could not lay hands on someone and command a physical illness to depart; but I could help broken lives and congregations find healing. When you work with a spiritual-gifts inventory, be prepared for surprises God may reveal.

Christians should consider other believers' insights as they seek to discover their spiritual gifts. We usually think we know ourselves better than anyone else knows us. But sometimes other Christians can see gifts in us that we have not seen. When the great Baptist preacher George W. Truett was young, he did not intend to devote his life to preaching the gospel. His church family, however, felt so strongly about his gifts that it determined to ordain him to the ministry. In time Truett accepted its assessment, and history records the great contributions he made to the Lord's work as a compassionate pastor and preacher.

God has given some Christians unusual discernment. These persons are able to help other Christians understand their gifts and identify ways God wants to use those gifts. We are wise to listen prayerfully when other believers feel impressed to identify gifts they see in us. At the same time, however, each of us is responsible to God for discovering and using our spiritual gifts. We cannot and should not depend solely on others to identify our gifts or God's will for our lives. Because every believer is a priest, God deals with each Christian on a personal, individual basis.

An effective way other Christians can help us develop our spiritual gifts is to affirm the gifts that have been identified. Watching the power of affirmation at work in a group that is studying spiritual gifts is thrilling. Christians who are unsure of their gifts or who feel unworthy about acknowledging their gifts are greatly encouraged when fellow Christians recognize and affirm their gifts. The Holy Spirit often moves in special ways in such an atmosphere of affirmation.

DOES GOD CALL ORDINARY CHRISTIANS?

When we think about getting on God's agenda, we must confront a concept among Christians that is both unbiblical and counterproductive to ministry. It is the belief, stated or implied, that God's call is reserved for special persons such as pastors, evangelists, missionaries, and other so-called full-time Christian workers. The concept is unbiblical because it is too narrow. Yes, God calls certain individuals to ministries that become their vocations, such as being a pastor or a missionary. But it is equally true that every Christian is called to full-time service for God's kingdom.

Both authors of this book are preachers. Both serve as pastors of local congregations. Both definitely feel that God called them as teenagers to preach the gospel. Both of us could relate the stories of our calls to preach and could recount the details of surrendering to those calls. We can affirm from our own experiences and from our studies of God's Word that God calls some Christians to vocational ministries. We can also affirm that God's call to vocational ministry is a prerequisite to performing those ministries and that no one should undertake such a ministry without having a sense of being called to it.

However, the Bible does not teach that only vocational ministers are called by God. On the contrary, the Scriptures lead us to the truth that God calls every Christian. When Peter spoke of our being a chosen generation and a kingdom of priests, his words were directed to all of the believers scattered over a wide area and not to the so-called clergy (see 1 Pet. 1:1; 2:9).

The division we make between clergy and laity has grown more from customs that emerged in church history than from biblical truth. When Constantine decreed that all Roman citizens were Christians by birth, this might have seemed a victory to Christians, who had formerly lived under the threat of persecution for their faith. But persons are not brought into relationship with God through governmental edict. Since everyone was declared by edict to be a Christian, the idea of a personal relationship with Christ was lost and, with it, the idea of God's call in individual lives. Only a select few, the church leaders, were believed to experience God's call. This faulty understanding of the Christian life led to a false distinction between clergy and laity, one the Scriptures do not support.

Martin Luther and other Reformation theologians reversed several hundred years' emphasis on this false distinction by highlighting the priesthood of believers. They taught that because every Christian is a priest, every Christian can experience God's call. In 1522 Luther preached a sermon in which he used the German word for calling, *beruf*, indicating that the word had the same meaning as *occupation*. This word had previously been used only for monks who were said to have been called by God. Luther's sermon challenged this idea. It was not the monk but the ordinary Christian who was called by God. Commenting on Luther's insight, Richard Broholm writes, "The genuine calling of God realizes itself within the world and its work, not in retreating from the world."[24] Roland Bainton, in his monumental work on Martin Luther, emphasizes the same truth: "In consequence the gospel could be exemplified only in the midst of secular callings, except that Luther refused to call them secular. As he had extended the priesthood of all believers, so likewise he extended the concept of divine calling, vocation, to all worthy occupations."[25]

Although we profess to believe in the priesthood of believers and in God's call in every Christian's life, our practice is sometimes inconsistent with our beliefs. Unfortunately, our actions imply the existence of three levels of Christians: the "called," meaning pastors and other vocational ministers; church leaders, such as deacons; and multitudes of "ordinary" believers, who do not think of themselves as called by God. The truth is that God calls some believers to very specific vocational ministries in the church, and God calls every believer to lifetime ministry in the world. Although we honor some callings with ordination, we fail to affirm the vocation of ministry to which every Christian has been called.

Jim was meeting with a group of fellow Christians that was discussing the implications of the doctrine of the priesthood of believers. When someone said that all Christians are in full-time Christian ministry, whatever their vocations, Jim's eyes welled with tears. He explained that when he was a freshman in college, he attended a summer conference on Christian discipleship, in which young adults were challenged to seek God's will for their lives. The counselor who supervised the young men in Jim's cabin announced to them that a commitment service would be held on the final night of the conference to recognize those who felt called to full-time Christian service. The counselor suggested that any young men who felt God's call should inform him before the service so that the pastor could recognize the commitments.

Jim had struggled with the feeling that God was calling him to become a high-school science teacher. As he experienced the Bible studies and worship during the conference, Jim became convinced of this call. As requested, he informed his cabin counselor that he wanted to participate in the commitment service.

When Friday night came, everyone gathered around a huge campfire. The names of those who had asked to be included in the service were called one at a time. As persons came forward and whispered to the pastor what they felt called to do, their decisions were announced to the group. Several felt called to be pastors, others to be missionaries. When Jim's turn came, he whispered to the pastor that he felt called to be a high-school science teacher. When Jim said this, the pastor frowned. Jim knew that something was wrong. Then the pastor said, with obvious irritation: "Jim, I'm sorry, but you made a mistake. This service is only for those who are committing themselves to full-time Christian service."

Relating his story in his late 60s, Jim explained: "For 45 years until my retirement, I worked as a science teacher in a very large urban high school. It was tough and demanding work and I think I had a real impact on the lives of a lot of young people. But until this day, I somehow felt that by choosing that vocation, I had denied Christ's call to ministry." Then Jim concluded, "My tears today are tears of joy to finally have my call to ministry affirmed as a faithful response to the call of Christ."[26]

God's call is not reserved for the few who do their work in the institutional church. God calls every Christian. The apostle elevated all honorable vocations to a sacred level when he wrote: "Whatever you do, work at it with all your heart, as working for the Lord, not for men, since you know you will receive an inheritance from the Lord as a reward. It is the Lord Christ you are serving" (Col. 3:23-24).

If we are to get on God's agenda, we must change the way we think about Christian calling. If God calls only religious professionals, the laity's role can be understood as supporting, giving, praying, and watching while "the called" carry out the church's ministry. It is unscriptural and impossible for so few to perform all the ministry required to reconcile a world of broken people to God. This is especially true of ministry evangelism. First Baptist Church in Leesburg, Florida, is able to carry on its many caring ministries because the pastor and other church leaders encourage the members to hear and heed God's call in their daily work and through involvement in the church's ministries. Hundreds of Christians in this church believe that God has called them to ministry evangelism. This pattern can and must be followed by any church that wants to minister to lost and hurting persons.

Phyllis Kamppi, a former director of the Women's Care Center at First Baptist Church, Leesburg, believes that God called her to this particular ministry. Phyllis testified to the way she experienced God's call:

> I think when we begin looking for a God-called ministry leader, we should extend our vision and not disqualify persons we feel certain He cannot use. That describes me. I could not have been a more unlikely candidate. After all, I had my life all neatly planned. My son, in his last year of high school, was joining the army. My mother, a semi-invalid, was coming to live with me. And I was getting married to a man I had known for six years.
>
> But a year before that, without any fanfare and certainly without my permission, the Lord had begun to prepare me for the day He was to call me. I was not even a Christian then; but my life, my goals, and my will were being changed. My life of sin was becoming intolerable, but I did not know what to do or where to go.
>
> I was saved one Sunday in September of 1989 as I sat alone in a pew at First Baptist, Leesburg, and gave to God all of the things I had thought I could not do without. I believe this total, unconditional surrender was essential for me to be able to

recognize—as well as accept—God's will for my life.

After I was saved, I began to do volunteer work at the Pregnancy-Care Center. For the first time, I led someone to the Lord. All of the other joys in my life paled by comparison, and I said, "Lord, if I could quit my job and have all of my other obligations taken care of, I'd do this for you full-time." God took me seriously and immediately began working out the details.

I found that God calls you in strange ways—even in the middle of choir practice. A woman I did not know leaned over and asked if I had considered becoming the director of the Women's Care Center. I did not even know it existed! I did the only thing I could do: I laughed. She did not. Ignoring my protests of other commitments of job and family, she asked me to pray about it.

I looked at my qualifications. Although I had been a nurse for 20 years, I questioned whether I would like working at the Women's Care Center. I found that God does not work that way. He did not ask me whether I was qualified; He asked whether I was willing. I realized that He would not call me to do something that would not make me happy. All I had to offer was a lifetime of sin and disobedience, but that's how He brings beauty from ashes.

Just as if I were looking down a long road, I turned around, and on each side of the road were the tragedies and sins—the worst parts—of my past life: alcoholism, drug addiction, prostitution, and rape. Yet I saw that God could use them for His glory. He could use the ashes of my life to help precious women free themselves from the bonds of sin and set them free. I was overwhelmed.

The only two qualifications for my calling were the only two I needed: I had faith in Him, and I was willing. As our pastor says: "God doesn't want our ability. He wants our availability. We could win this world to Jesus if we would all join together in faith and say, 'Yes, Lord, send me.' "

All of God's people are called to ministry. Ministry evangelism depends on church members who are willing to get on God's agenda by taking this call seriously. The New Testament affirms the calling of all of God's people to serve Him as ministers. Then those who are called to vocational ministry in the church can concentrate on encouraging and equipping God's people for the "works of service" to which God has called them (see Eph. 4:11-12).

---

[1]Leonard Griffith, *We Have This Ministry* (Waco: Word, 1973), 30.
[2]Ibid.
[3]Ibid., 32–33.
[4]Findley B. Edge, *A Quest for Vitality in Religion* (Nashville: Broadman Press, 1963), 133–34.
[5]Ibid., 136.
[6]Ibid.
[7]Ibid.
[8]Ibid., 137.
[9]Findley B. Edge, "The Meaning of Ministry" in *LAOS: All the People of God*, ed. Fisher Humphreys and Thomas A. Kinchen (New Orleans: New Orleans Baptist Theological Seminary, 1984), 70.
[10]William Pinson, "Ministry Now" in *LAOS: All the People of God*, 111.
[11]Delos Miles, "Church Social Work and Evangelism as Partners" in *Evangelism in the 21st Century*, ed. Thom S. Rainer (Wheaton: Harold Shaw Publishers, 1989), 55.
[12]Ibid.
[13]Darrell W. Robinson, *Total Church Life* (Nashville: Broadman Press, 1985), 112.
[14]Drummond, "A Theology of the Laity: Spiritual Gifts" in *LAOS: All the People of God*, 46.
[15]Edge, "The Meaning of Ministry" in *LAOS: All the People of God*, 72–73.
[16]Robinson, *Total Church Life*, 111.
[17]Lewis Drummond, "A Theology of the Laity: Spiritual Gifts" in *LAOS: All the People of God*, 48.
[18]J. W. MacGorman, *The Gifts of the Spirit* (Nashville: Broadman Press, 1974), 29.
[19]Ebbie C. Smith and Bill Latham, *Member's Booklet/Individual Study Guide, Discovering Your Spiritual Gifts* (Equipping Center module), rev. ed. (Nashville: Convention Press, 1981), 11.
[20]Ken Hemphill, *The Official Rule Book for the New Church Game* (Nashville: Broadman Press, 1990), 154.
[21]Drummond, "A Theology of the Laity: Spiritual Gifts" in *LAOS: All the People of God*, 50.
[22]Hemphill, *The Official Rule Book for the New Church Game*, 157–58.
[23]Ibid., 156.
[24]Richard Broholm, "The Call to Holy Worldliness: The Unfinished Reformation Agenda" in *LAOS: All the People of God*, 63.
[25]Roland Bainton, *Here I Stand* (Nashville: Abingdon Press, 1950), 233.
[26]Broholm, "The Call to Holy Worldliness: The Unfinished Reformation Agenda" in *LAOS: All the People of God*, 58–59.

6

Living with a Ministry Outlook

THIS BOOK HAS FOCUSED on the biblical and theological truths that undergird ministry to hurting persons. This ministry, performed in the name of Jesus Christ, is intended to lead persons into saving relationships with God. We have been reminded that God's heart has always been filled with love and concern for hurting, broken persons. We have seen that the church is the body of Christ that has been called out to love as Christ loved and to minister redemptively as He ministered. We have learned that the Holy Spirit gifts members of the body of Christ for ministry and have considered every believer's responsibility to discover, develop, and employ spiritual gifts to minister and witness to others. We have also seen that members of the body of Christ must be nurtured, cared for, and sometimes healed of deep personal hurts if the church is to do Christ's work effectively in the world.

First Baptist Church of Leesburg, Florida, has served as our model for ministry evangelism. We have seen many examples of lives that have been redeemed and transformed through this great church's ministry and witness. With more than 70 ministries, First Baptist Church is a model for caring that brings persons into saving relationships with the Lord Jesus Christ.

For churches like First Baptist, Leesburg, ministry evangelism is more than a program; it is a way of looking at the Christian life and the church's work. In reality, ministry evangelism is a Christian lifestyle, not an activity in which to take part. Congregations and individuals across the world are discovering how to live with a ministry outlook. The following true stories are only a few of many that could be told.

MINISTRY EVANGELISM IN ACTION

Harmony Baptist Church in Saint Louis, Missouri, has discovered a unique ministry opportunity in the heart of the city. Really, it is more accurate to say that a unique ministry has discovered the congregation of Harmony Baptist Church. This church is not a large church. The average

Sunday School attendance is about one hundred. Harmony Baptist Church has ministered in its area of the city for the past 40 years. Like most churches, it has provided worship experiences, Bible study, discipleship training, and Christian fellowship for its members. For many years the church has ministered to its ethnically diverse neighborhood through food distribution and a literacy program. Recently, however, God brought new life to the church through a unique ministry opportunity.

A group in the church was studying *Experiencing God: Knowing and Doing the Will of God.* One unit relates a story about a church that was challenged to minister when a German-speaking man appeared at the door. Harmony Baptist Church had a similar experience when a Haitian man visited a worship service. A recent immigrant, he spoke only Haitian French but somehow communicated that he was a Christian looking for a place to worship and minister. After a time of difficult communication church members offered to teach the man the English language. In time other Haitians came to the church to learn the language of their adopted home.

What began as a ministry to one man, then to a few Haitians, has become a full-fledged mission to Haitian immigrants. What began as language training has grown to include a full range of ministries. The church provides food, shelter, furniture, clothing, and other social services in cooperation with community agencies and other Christian groups. Efforts are made to help these new residents find jobs and homes. More importantly, the church is learning to minister to these persons' spiritual needs. Although the two congregations have separate worship services, they interact frequently. Members of the original Harmony Baptist congregation teach the language classes, provide food and clothing, and offer friendship to the members of the new congregation. Opportunities for joint worship using both languages are frequent. The church has truly found new life in this ministry.

The purpose of ministry evangelism is to introduce persons to the Lord Jesus Christ. The Haitian mission of Harmony Baptist Church actually baptizes more new converts than the mother church. Pastor Rick Lay explains: "These people have felt needs. As they experience the love of Christ in the meeting of those needs, many of them come to know Him."

An important part of the story of this ministry in Saint Louis is that God initiated it. The church did not plan its significant ministry to Haitian immigrants. Instead, God presented this opportunity when a needy man appeared at the door. The leaders and people of Harmony Baptist responded to the challenge with love.

Second Baptist Church of Little Rock, Arkansas, has a long history of ministry to persons with various needs. This great inner-city church has chosen to stay downtown to minister to persons' needs. The residents of Little Rock know that the church cares because of ministries like the following.

• The church ministers to needy children through the Dame Memorial Fund. Years ago a Mr. Dame came to Little Rock in need and turned to Second Baptist Church for help. The church ministered to him and helped him through that difficult time. Mr. Dame later became a successful businessman but never forgot the church that ministered to him, leaving the church a large amount of money to be used to help children in the inner city. The interest on that money, about seven thousand dollars a year, is used at Christmas to buy clothing and gifts for children who would otherwise have no gifts. These children are matched with church families, who take them shopping to select what they need and want.

• Another member of Second Baptist Church remembers the embarrassment of starting the first grade without necessary clothing because his family was very poor. This man, who has also enjoyed financial success, contributes money each fall to fund a program the church calls RALY, Reach and Love Youth. Through this program the church provides school clothing for inner-city children who are beginning the first grade.

• Recently, this Little Rock congregation decided to respond in love to the growing problem of AIDS. An AIDS Care Team accepted the responsibility of ministering to persons with the dread disease. This intensive ministry matches team members with HIV-positive persons. The consistent ministry of kindness, care, and spiritual help continues as long as the patient lives.

• The church also sponsors block parties for persons in the inner city. Church members supply food, entertainment, and friendship; and a Christian witness permeates the whole event. At a recent party inner-city children were enlisted to paint appropriate graffiti on large panels, which became the backdrop for a musical presented later. The young artists were invited to the concert to see their art on display.

Ministry is offered by Second Baptist Church, Little Rock, unconditionally. However, all of the church's ministry is done in Jesus' name as a witness to His love and redemptive power.

Clyde McCants was hurting when God's providence brought him to Millbrook Baptist Church in Aiken, South Carolina. An experience with a church he pastored had ended badly, and Clyde wondered whether God could ever use his life again. The members of Millbrook Baptist put their arms around McCants and ministered to him in many ways. One day when McCants was discussing some of his pain with Millbrook's pastor, Jim Rivers, the pastor mentioned a mission of the church in Rock Cave, West Virginia. He asked Clyde if he would like to preach at the tiny mission of seven members. McCants eagerly agreed to go.

McCants traveled to the mountains of central West Virginia to the little village of Rock Cave. He was so captivated by the beauty of the mountains that he could hardly hold his car on the curves of the two-lane mountain highway. When he met the members of the mission, he was even more impressed. They were equally impressed with McCants, soon asking him to become their pastor. He accepted the call and began his work as the pastor of New Covenant Baptist Church of Rock Cave in January 1984.

Clyde McCants faced quite a challenge in his new home and ministry. Many persons in the little village and in the surrounding area were trapped in poverty, much of which was created by the failure of the coal-mining industry. Many persons were on welfare. Alcoholism and drug abuse were rampant. Family problems such as spousal and child abuse were commonplace. Divorce was frequent. Many persons, adults and children alike, were unable to read. Hope was not easy to find.

The past 11 years have held many miracles for the pastor and his people. McCants soon saw the need for the food ministry that had already been established and was assisting 33 families. The average family in the Rock Creek area consists of about 4 persons, with an average income less than $250 a month, including food stamps. The church now distributes more than six thousand pounds of food each month to about 250 families. Church members actively participate in the food distribution, including gospel tracts with the food. Government programs provide much of the food, with church members and the Home Mission Board of the Southern Baptist Convention supplying the remainder.

The need for food is only one need that Pastor McCants and New Covenant Baptist Church try to meet. The need for a clothing ministry was also immediately apparent, but the church had room for only a clothes closet. One day McCants's father-in-law offered the use of a building for a clothes ministry. That same day a large shipment of clothing to be used in

Rock Cave arrived from a church in Louisiana. By God's providence and perfect timing, the clothes ministry was born. Today this ministry flourishes. With the help of construction crews from churches in other states, buildings have been erected on the church property to house both the food and the clothing ministries.

Another tremendous need in Rock Cave was to teach persons to read. A literacy program was begun when a 56-year-old church member needed to learn to read to take a test for a driver's license. A branch program from nearby Buckhannon now helps many adults learn to read. One reason the church's literacy ministry is important is so that the area's people can read the Bible and the Christian literature the church distributes.

When persons in the community began coming to Clyde McCants for counseling with problems he felt unqualified to deal with, he began to pray for help. The Home Mission Board of the Southern Baptist Convention referred him to the HCA River Park Hospital in Huntington, West Virginia, which agreed to work with the church to provide a free counseling service in Rock Cave. Marlena Maynard, a licensed professional counselor, travels to Rock Cave twice a week to work with clients on a wide range of personal and family problems. Because Maynard is a committed Christian who feels that God has called her to work in Rock Cave, she provides counseling without charge. She uses biblical principles along with sound counseling practices to help persons cope with their problems.

Children's needs led the church to house a Head Start program. Because the federal government funds this program, the church cannot practice overt evangelism. However, the program has provided opportunities to minister to several families of the children who are enrolled.

Clyde McCants preaches, teaches, and practices ministry. He and his wife work tirelessly to meet human need and to bring the hope of the gospel to persons in the area. Millbrook Baptist Church in Aiken, South Carolina, faithfully supports the work of New Covenant Baptist Church in Rock Cave and its pastor. When eight thousand dollars was needed to prepare the building for the Head Start program, Millbrook provided the money and labor to make it possible. Many other churches in several states have taken part in Rock Cave's ministry by sending cash gifts, clothing, mission teams, and construction workers. McCants views this help as God's miracles to keep the work going.

The pastor and the church continue to dream big dreams. Recently, a tragedy in the community gave birth to one of those dreams. A young girl who was regularly beaten by her drunken father was ordered by her abused mother to shoot him. The girl hated her father, so she did as she was told.

Following the tragedy, the child's mother was sent to prison. The little girl had no place to go except to relatives, who were not likely to treat her better than her abusive father did. McCants could do nothing. Now he is waiting on God's miracle that will make possible a children's home where such children can be helped. Area judges have encouraged the idea. McCants believes that God will provide the means for developing this ministry, just as He has provided for the other ministries.

The pastor also dreams of establishing a training center to teach unemployed persons skills needed to escape the welfare trap. He considers food and clothing only temporary relief for a more serious problem. Only if persons are given hope for escaping despair can they be permanently helped.

The ministries of New Covenant Baptist Church are given unconditionally. Persons are helped because they have needs, but the help is always given in the name of Jesus Christ. McCants believes that evangelizing someone who has an empty stomach is impossible. He has learned that we cannot expect hurting persons to believe that God loves them unless we are willing to minister to their hurts. The pastor wonders if needy persons believe that God prefers the rich over the poor when they see churches spend all of their resources on themselves—on buildings, furnishings, and property. His ministry in a very difficult place is making a difference and serves as a challenge to all of us.

Tens of thousands of older citizens live in nursing homes and other care facilities. Many others are homebound. Although many receive excellent care, others receive hardly any care. Some are regularly visited by loving family members and friends. Others spend their days in the prison of loneliness. All of these older persons have spiritual needs. Some have been spiritual giants in their churches but now find their spiritual needs neglected. Some are lost and alone, desperately needing to know Jesus. All of them need persons to care for them, pray for them, and share God's Word with them.

Maurice Cooper, a longtime employee of the North Carolina Baptist Convention, has always had a special place in his heart for older persons, especially those who are homebound or in nursing homes. Cooper realized that such persons need visits and attention, but he believed that they need more. He began to think about these older persons' love for the Bible. Some of them taught it to others for many years. They lived by its promises and loved the God it reveals. But now many of them are unable to read the Bible for themselves. Cooper wondered what could be done to share God's Word with these special persons. His thinking and praying about this need led to the development of The Samaritan Touch, a ministry to older adults who can no longer attend church or study the Bible for themselves.

Cooper compiled a collection of Scriptures titled *Let the Bible Speak: Bible Passages for Special People.*[1] The ministry involves giving the book to the older person, then returning regularly to read comforting Bible promises and passages to the patient. The visitor stays an appropriate length of time, considering the person's physical needs, and prays before leaving. The older person might be asked to pray if she wishes.

Sharing God's Word with disabled, neglected, or lonely persons is a needed ministry. While this ministry is primarily intended for older persons who are already Christians, it can also be used to introduce unsaved patients to Christ. A number of churches and individuals use this excellent book. For example, Mae Britt, 83 years old, has used copies of the book with 50 persons in nursing homes. The ministry can also be performed by reading from other books or from the Bible.

Of this caregiving ministry Maurice Cooper says: "Being a caregiver is a personal ministry to a special group of persons. These persons need you because they are frequently ignored or left out of society. As a caregiver you can give your time and yourself to others. The only prerequisite for this ministry is simple compassion. Your ministry of presence is often a clear representation of Christ's presence and care in their lives."

~~

Each Tuesday night Sunday School rooms at East Side Baptist Church in Fort Smith, Arkansas, become doctors' examining rooms; medical labs; and offices for nurses, social workers, and nutritionists. The transformation is part of the church's unique ministry to meet a specific need in the community. The Agape Prenatal Clinic offers free medical care for expectant mothers who are unmarried, indigent, or without health insurance. Veta Rush, the coordinator of the clinic volunteers, schedules appointments for the women from a telephone in her home. Local doctors and other health professionals donate their time, and 20 volunteers work each week at the clinic. The first night 13 women visited the clinic. The number quickly grew to about 30 each week.

The clinic was the dream of Randy Feezell, a practicing obstetrician and gynecologist and a member of East Side Baptist Church. He comments: "We've had every affirmation that this is what we're supposed to be doing. We've gotten all of the equipment we needed, and the church has provided a good group of willing volunteers."

Many women who visit the clinic bring their children with them, providing an opportunity for the church to minister to the whole family. Volunteers provide activities and Bible study through which the children experience love, study God's Word, and take the Word home through Bible-study leaflets. Mothers and children are invited to return to the church for Sunday School.

According to East Side's pastor, John Marshall, the Agape Prenatal Clinic has helped church members become more sensitive to community needs. The church is now studying other ways to minister. Pastor Marshall comments: "We have a strong feeling at East Side that the church too often abdicates its responsibility to the government. As a result, we've turned over the greatest opportunity to launch evangelism and penetrate the world in which we live."[2]

~~

What is Saturday Sunday School? The members of First Baptist Church, Leesburg, Florida, are happy to answer that question. Saturday Sunday School is an effort to reach boys and girls with the gospel of the Lord Jesus Christ. Designed for children in kindergarten through the sixth grade, Saturday Sunday School mostly attracts boys and girls from lower socioeconomic housing areas. Because many have no means of transportation, the church has purchased buses to bring them to the church each Saturday.

The director of Saturday Sunday School also assigns workers specific geographic areas in which they are to enlist children for the program. These workers visit in homes, get to know the parents, minister to the family, and witness at every opportunity. The program allows tremendous opportunities for ministry and evangelism among persons who are not likely to attend church on Sunday. The number of children has grown to several hundred each Saturday. Plans call for expanding Saturday Sunday School to include youth in grades 7 through 12.

~~

Joseph Burwell is not a typical Baptist pastor. Nor is Fellowship Baptist Church a typical Baptist church. This young pastor and his church have discovered a unique ministry in Kearneysville, West Virginia, where Burwell was born and reared. Foxglen, the community where Fellowship Baptist Church makes its home, was considered "the wrong side of the tracks" when he was growing up. This multiethnic neighborhood has more than its share of crack houses and social deterioration that drug trafficking always brings. Foxglen is made up of 65 percent single-parent families, with 40 percent of the residents being ethnics. The community has seven hundred residents under the age of 18, many of whom are parents. For years there was no church presence. Almost none of the residents ever had a connection with a church.

In October of 1990 Joseph Burwell accepted the challenge of coming to Foxglen as the pastor of the mission that would become Fellowship Baptist Church. The beginning was not very promising. The mission had 13 members and met in a building that had formerly been used as a massage parlor in a strip mall. Next door to the mission was a bar that featured strip shows. Crack dealers peddled their wares in the parking lot. The inside of the building was no better than its surroundings. Broken-down furniture on a greasy carpet greeted worshipers. But soon the little group of Christians cleaned the carpet and painted the walls.

Ministry has never been easy for the pastor and members of Fellowship Baptist Church. They saw the need to improve the community itself as their first step. The residents of Foxglen did not know one another. Every house had a locked gate. Residents worked outside the community but were afraid to venture beyond their gates at night because of crime, especially trafficking in crack. The streets were full of potholes, and crack dealers stopped cars in the streets. The only place of business was a convenience store, outside of which drugs were openly sold. No street signs existed; when the police and fire departments were called, they usually could not locate the problem.

Burwell and the church led the way in community improvement. Community events such as an Easter-egg hunt were planned. Community meetings were held to help residents get to know one another. The church became a liaison to community-improvement agencies. A Boy Scout troop was organized. The church started a community newspaper to publicize events and to bring persons together.

At first the church ignored the ever-present drug dealers, hoping that they might influence them without confrontation. However, when the situation threatened the safety of persons attending the church, Burwell took action. Each night from 8:00 until midnight he watched the parking lot, took the tag numbers of those doing business with the crack dealers, and turned them in to the authorities. This bold action began to make a difference. Several drug raids were carried out. Gradually, the drug dealers left the community.

Today Foxglen is a better place to live. Street signs are visible. Residents are taking pride in the community and are cleaning up the trash. Persons are getting to know one another. The community has initiated programs that are improving everyone's quality of life. Recently, the community was chosen for a grant after competing with 1,500 other communities. At the center of this progress are the witness and influence of Joseph Burwell and the members of Fellowship Baptist Church.

The church eventually acquired property and built a multipurpose building to house the congregation—a gymnasium with a worship area and classroom space. The church's ministry is enhanced by a building that looks more like a community center than a church. Residents of Foxglen would probably not come to a church building, but they are likely to come to activities at a warehouse, as Burwell describes it. The church focuses its ministry on children. In a community with no playgrounds or children's programs, the church is making a difference by providing planned activities for boys and girls who might otherwise get into trouble. Many of these children have accepted Christ, opening doors of ministry to their parents.

Joseph Burwell once visited a man who assured him that he had no need for a church and emphatically promised that he would never attend the church services. The pastor asked if the man's son could attend, and the father gave his permission. When the boy was chosen to play an instrument in the Christmas program, the father came to observe, although he barely came inside the building and left as soon as his son's part was over. At a later program the father was asked to videotape the program. He came, stood near the door with his camera, and left as soon as he could. Later, when the man's son participated in an Easter presentation of the Lord's Supper, the father asked if he could videotape it. This time he moved around the building to get the best camera angle, even coming near the stage. At the conclusion of the program the father put down his camera and came forward in tears to accept Christ. Today this man, a growing Christian, is part of a training program for prospective deacons.

In addition to its ministries to children, Fellowship Baptist Church serves many community needs. Last year the church fed over three hundred families. When a family suffers a crisis such as a fire, the church routinely serves as the collection-and-distribution point for the needed help.

Burwell is heavily involved in crisis ministry in the neighborhood, working between 50 and 60 hours a week as an officer on the ambulance squad. He is also the chaplain of the fire department and a deputy with the sheriff's department. These tasks involve him in almost every crisis in the community. Often, Burwell's first contact with a family stems from a crisis, enabling him to enter homes in which he would never be welcomed as a pastor. Persons who never intend to attend church have grown to expect his presence when trouble comes.

Because most of the church members are new Christians, Burwell nurtures them to help them find their places of service in the church's ministries. He calls his ministry a teaching ministry more than a preaching ministry, understanding his pastoral role as an equipper of other believers for the ministries to which God has called them. He views his ministry in light of Ephesians 4, with his main responsibility being to prepare members for ministry. While Sunday-morning services are traditional, on Sunday evenings he discusses questions members have raised. Members frequently study *Survival Kit for Christians* and *Basics for Baptists*. In addition, the Church Study Course plan[3] is used to disciple new Christians, most of whom come from non-Christian backgrounds. Believers are led to discover their spiritual gifts by means of spiritual-gifts inventories. When members feel called to particular ministries, they are encouraged and permitted to develop the ministries. Burwell has found that letting go of ministries and permitting his church members to take the lead are sometimes difficult but important steps. Ministry ideas that do not work are not viewed as defeat. Instead, the pastor helps members evaluate their experiences and find ways to minister more effectively.

Joseph Burwell serves in a difficult place. He is paid very little, and he works long hours in other jobs. But the happiness of being where God wants him to be makes it worthwhile. The young pastor sees no conflict between evangelism and social ministry. He knows that spiritual needs are primary and that only the changes Christ brings can make the ultimate difference in a person's life. But he knows, too, that many times the only way the gospel gets a hearing is in the context of caring for persons' pain and brokenness.

Now It Is Your Turn

A phrase often heard in the business world is *paradigm shift*. A paradigm is a set of assumptions governing the way we do things. In the context of this study it refers to the assumptions that regulate the ways churches minister.

One such paradigm is what Bill Hull calls the pulpit-dependent church. To this type of church, *outreach* means bringing persons to church to hear the pastor preach.[4] The problem with this model is that it is no longer effective as a means of bringing persons to Christ. This argument does not diminish the importance of biblical preaching but stresses that preaching alone, no matter how brilliant, will not bring large numbers of persons to the Savior, because unsaved persons are not usually eager to travel to the church building to hear a sermon.

Hull insists that the church needs a paradigm shift: "We need to shift away from the hermetically sealed pulpit with no real life in it toward the leadership pulpit." He adds, "The church must make the shift to multi-dimensional outreach and evangelism."[5] What is called for, according to Hull, is leadership ministry. He identifies several crucial elements in this type of ministry:

• Teach/preach.
• Develop a strategy and distill it into a vision statement.
• Cast the vision.
• Engineer change.
• Manage persons—getting work done through others.
• Manage conflict.[6]

Although each element could be the subject of an entire study, the crucial point is that pastors and other church leaders who want to reach persons in this complex world cannot hope to do so without understanding that preaching alone will not accomplish that goal. Church leaders must be willing to lead God's people to become the ministers God intends for them to be and to involve them in evangelism and ministry. This is exactly what ministry evangelism is all about—God's people reaching out in love to meet needs and share Christ.

Pastors and other leaders must operate from a vision for meeting persons' needs and bringing them to the Lord Jesus Christ. George Barna admonishes us to "realize that true ministry begins with vision. For a Christian leader—that is, an individual God has chosen to move His people forward—vision is not to be regarded as an option. It is the insight that instructs the leader and directs his or her path." Barna concludes, "If for whatever reason, you are attempting to lead God's people without God's vision for your ministry, you are simply playing a dangerous game. It is a game that neither pleases God nor satisfies people."[7]

Ministry evangelism must begin with church leaders. Pastors and other leaders must come to the point that they are no longer satisfied with business as usual in the church. They must hunger to make a real difference in a broken world. They must seek God's leadership and power. They must be willing to take the risks that change can bring. From this hunger and willingness God can bring renewal to His church and glory to His name.

Pastor Charles Roesel and the members of First Baptist Church, Leesburg, Florida, have served as the inspiration for this study. Charles is a warm-hearted, dedicated minister of the gospel who has led the church to reach out in love to thousands of persons. He is a visionary leader who equips others for the work to which God calls them—the work of ministry evangelism. As coauthors, we wanted to close this study by asking you to listen in on a conversation we shared. Our prayer is that as Charles reveals his heart for ministry evangelism, God will give you a vision of and excitement for meeting needs and sharing Christ in your area of influence. We also hope that you will act on your new commitment by implementing some of the numerous ministry ideas in these chapters and in appendix 2 or others suggested by needs in your community.

Don: Charles, what do you mean by *ministry evangelism?*

Charles: Ministry evangelism reaches persons by loving them in their hurts. This means loving persons not as prospects but as persons and dealing with their perceived needs—the needs that are the most pressing as far as they are concerned. The purpose of this ministry is to make them aware of their deepest need, which is Jesus Christ. The tragedy is that many times they are so immersed in their hurts and immediate problems, they are not thinking about spiritual matters. As we help them deal with their hurts and as they sense that we genuinely love them, they may become willing to listen when we talk to them about Jesus. We have gained their confidence by caring for them and by ministering to them.

Don: If you had to choose particular biblical passages on which this concept is built, which would you choose?

Charles: The passage in Matthew 25 is the theme of my life and the greatest ministry-evangelism text. It is a picture of the final exam. Jesus says, " 'I was hungry and you gave me something to eat, I was thirsty and you gave me something to drink, I was a stranger and you invited me in, I needed clothes and you clothed me, I was sick and you looked after me, I was in prison and you came to visit me' " (vv. 35-36). Helping hurting persons is a divine mandate.

We know that God intends for us to reach persons for Jesus Christ because the first word He gave to His disciples was " 'Follow me, ... and I will make you fishers of men' " (Mark 1:17). The last word He gave to them was " 'You will receive power after that the Holy Spirit comes on you; and you will be my witnesses in Jerusalem, and in all Judea and Samaria, and to the ends of the earth' " (Acts 1:8). Jesus' first and last commands apply to us as much as to the disciples. These commands ought to represent our first concern.

Many passages, such as the account of the woman at the well, indicate that Jesus related on the level of persons' needs and then made them realize their eternal needs. Other passages portray Jesus healing persons and, in the process, making them aware of their sin and their need for spiritual healing.

Don: So ministry evangelism is caring for persons, but it goes beyond that.

Charles: It goes far beyond that because if we meet only their physical needs without meeting their eternal needs, we have failed to give them what they need most of all—salvation through the Lord Jesus Christ.

Don: Your ministry demonstrates that you are a very caring person. What early experiences brought you to this point in your ministry?

Charles: First, from early in my life my father and mother were very godly persons who believed in a practical Christianity. They really were not impressed with persons who talked the faith but did not walk it, who talked about the hungry but did not feed them, who talked about the hurting but did not minister. I can remember my mother and father taking persons into our home—persons with all kinds of hurts. Our table was always set for strangers as well as for the family. Mama never prepared just for us. I was reared in an environment in which my mother and father constantly reached out to others; so I understood when I accepted Christ, from my parents' model, that Christianity is something you do, not just something you profess or feel.

When I was a seminary student, I spent two years training in a psychiatric institution and came to feel deeply for the hurting persons who suffered mentally, emotionally, and spiritually. I spent hours with them and learned to love the walking wounded. I also worked as a counselor at a juvenile-detention home for young, troubled boys. Once I was teaching the Lord's Prayer and began by saying, "God is our Heavenly Father, and He is like our father." With my background that sounded fine. But one boy stood up and shouted, "If God is like my father, I don't want anything to do with Him!" and stormed out of the room. Then I glimpsed, in part, the depth of bitterness and pain in the human heart.

From there I went to a mining community in eastern Kentucky, where persons were hurting in unbelievable ways. Strikes had lasted for years, and finally people quit using coal; so a depression occurred during the '60s in that area. I ministered to a lot of poor persons, driving into the hills and up riverbeds with an old truck to take children to Vacation Bible School. There too I learned to relate to all kinds of persons and to love them in their hurts.

When I was called to First Baptist Church of Zephyrhills, Florida, I became aware that girls who were removed from homes where they had been molested, raped, and abused were imprisoned simply because no other place existed to house or protect them. We started a teenage girls' home and ministered to about 350 young women over a 3½-year period. I really developed a heart for the hurting through that ministry.

Also early in my ministry there we started a coffee-house ministry to reach hippies and yippies for the Lord Jesus. We gave them an old house and let them paint it as they wanted to. What they did to it was awful, but it became a means of identification with them. We reached many young persons for Christ through that ministry.

Don: It sounds as if the Holy Spirit used a variety of experiences from your boyhood through your pastorates to bring you to where you are today, Charles. I want to ask you about the church where you serve now. I have visited First Baptist Church, Leesburg, several times, and it is an experience just to walk on the grounds. I could sense and feel the love in the church family. Many church members are strongly committed to ministry. But I understand that maybe it was not always that way. This must have been a process of growth for your church, just as it was for you. Would you share how things got started at First Baptist Church?

Charles: This was a dignified but dying downtown church 18 years ago. The average Sunday School attendance had declined from four hundred to less than three hundred. Baptisms had totaled less than 20 a year for the past 10 years, and the church had been divided over that. People told me: "Don't go to First Baptist; that's a preacher-killer church. They are hard on preachers; you won't last long." When I first arrived, I thought they were right. The first Sunday service was very cold, so I suggested at the end of the service that we join hands and sing "Sweet, Sweet Spirit." That afternoon a deacon called me and asked whether the church was becoming charismatic. The next Sunday I apologized and admitted that the Bible says nothing about holding hands. Instead, I suggested that we greet one another with a holy kiss. The congregation laughed, and the ice began thawing some. But change was very slow, and much resistance was evident.

When we wanted to start a Children's Shelter, for example, a man offered to give us the property, and another man offered to give us the money. Yet when the proposal was presented, the church approved it by only 51 percent. I responded: "We cannot start a ministry like that! We need to wait." Later, when we began ministry evangelism, a small faction resisted every move. One man said, "I don't want my family to have to walk past transients on our way to the sanctuary." That kind of response was not unusual. But because of fine lay leadership we went ahead and started the Rescue Mission. Being inexperienced, we made a lot of mistakes. But step-by-step we learned, and the ministries were used to touch lives for the Lord Jesus. We now have more than 70 ministries and have ministered to thousands of persons through them.

Don: How are leaders enlisted for service in these ministries?

Charles: Our best staff ministers have come up through the ranks. Persons have been saved, have been nurtured, and have matured in Christ here in our own family to become leaders in ministry evangelism. God has raised up outstanding staff members from the heart of our own fellowship.

Don: This ministry also requires numerous volunteer workers in the church. Are members willing to get involved in the ministries?

Charles: Our members fill 1,400 volunteer positions. Saturday Sunday School alone has 70 workers, our two-week Vacation Bible School requires over 300 workers, and all of our ministries have volunteers who give literally thousands of hours every month. I am convinced that the church will never move forward unless laypersons are allowed the freedom to do what God has called them to do. Many churches feel that when something needs to be done, they must hire someone to do it. We do not do that. For example, our Homebound Ministry is conducted solely by volunteers. It began when a couple recruited 400 members to minister to 400 shut-ins and then trained them.

Don: If a member of your church feels God's leadership in a ministry direction, how would he start that ministry and involve others?

Charles: That person would come to me or to Art Ayris, my associate, and would share what is on his heart. Then we would thoroughly investigate the proposal to determine whether to do it. We often find that the person to whom God has spoken about the ministry is the one God has chosen to lead the ministry. Some persons are not spiritually, morally, or emotionally qualified to provide ministry leadership; but if they are, we turn them loose. It is amazing what God can do with an individual who has the gifts, heart, and dedication. For instance, the couple who began the Homebound Ministry did so from love and commitment. When persons are really in love with Jesus and are excited about serving Him, that love and excitement are contagious. Recruiting workers is usually easy because persons enjoy the company of leaders who are committed to their work.

Don: Would you equate what you have described with being called by God to a work?

Charles: I believe that when God lays a burden on someone's heart, that is a calling. Giving a person a burden is not the only way He calls the person to ministry, but it is one of the primary ways He does so.

Don: If a church is going to win persons to Christ through a caring ministry, what is the pastor's role?

Charles: It is imperative that he not only teach it and preach it but also model it. A pastor must be on the front lines. For example, if I have a visitation program, I must be present at the visitation time. God has called us to lead by example. A pastor should lead not by guilt but by loving leadership. He should be out front saying, "I am with you; let's go together." Pastors should also take some of the most difficult tasks instead of giving them to our laypersons to let them know that we are willing to suffer, to pay the price, to do whatever is necessary to win the world to Jesus. If we don't model ministry, it does not matter how much we teach it and preach it. They are not going to do it.

A pastor also has an important role in encouraging persons doing worthy work for the Lord. If the pastor wants all the credit, all the praise, all the spotlight, he will get it; but that's all he will have. He won't have a ministering church, and he won't reach persons for the Lord. Jesus has to get the glory, and we have to be willing to hold up others the Lord is using to do His work—hold them up before the congregation and encourage them.

Don: How does your preaching challenge and encourage members to reach out and touch hurting and lost persons?

Charles: I have come to believe very strongly in what I call confessional preaching. As I preach God's Word, I am very honest in sharing my shortcomings so that listeners can identify with me as a real person. For example, I have shared many times something I am ashamed to share: when transients sought help at our church, I wanted to give them as little as possible to get them as far down the road as possible so that they would be someone else's responsibility. When I share that, many of them nod as if to say, "I have felt that way myself." Then I tell them that God almost verbally said to me, "While you are trying to get members to go out and knock on doors, persons are knocking on your door every day whose needs you are not meeting." I asked God to forgive my attitude of not wanting to be involved. I didn't want to confront someone who was hurting because it was very discouraging; and until the Lord dealt firmly with me, I wasn't willing to pay the price. I share these matters with my members. They identify with their pastor, and together we grow.

I have found that members love the pastor more if he is honest and that they forgive his shortcomings. They come to him more readily if they know that he fails and has weaknesses, struggles, and frustrations. Honesty removes the wall of intimidation.

Don: Is it true that during the worship service persons come forward to pray about their burdens and needs?

Charles: Yes, and the origin of this practice was providential. One Sunday I knew what many members felt because I had suffered with them. Seeing the pain on their faces, I said: "I feel the Spirit leading to allow a time for you to come forward if you have special hurts. Other members and I want to pray for you." I expected 5 or 10 members to come forward. Instead, persons filled the aisles and the front of the church seeking a miracle, a word, and encouragement from God. I recognized that if that many hurting members were willing to bring their needs to God, we ought to provide that opportunity every Sunday.

Don: What does your church do to equip your members for ministry?

Charles: If we don't keep our own family healthy, our spiritual family in Christ, it will not be able to minister to others. In our church we minister to the total person. We have programs for physical fitness just as we have programs for spiritual and mental fitness. Furthermore, we believe that LIFE® courses are one of the finest series God has given our family. We use *MasterLife, Parenting by Grace, WiseCounsel: Skills for Lay Counseling, Experiencing God: Knowing and Doing the Will of God,* and other courses to equip our members in discipleship and for ministry.

We also minister to our members' financial needs. When members get into financial trouble, we offer not only financial help but also financial counsel so that they won't fall back into destructive patterns. We have found that ministering to, loving, and encouraging the church family develop effective ministers and witnesses.

Don: How does your church fund its wide range of ministries and still keep the church functioning?

Charles: A church should start by using what it already has. We began with what we had and in the past 18 years purchased 19 parcels of land. Most of these parcels had houses on them that we used for ministries. But because the ministries have grown, we are building a new ministry village that will include a new Rescue Mission, Women's Shelter, Children's Shelter, Teen Shelter, Pregnancy-Care Center, Benevolence Center, and others. The Lord has provided this money in amazing ways. For example, a quiet, godly layman in our church told me that we needed another parcel of land on the block where we were planning to build the ministry village and indicated that he would buy it for us. The owner would not sell it, so the man committed the $100,000 to the Lord for this village. Then a godly lady offered us a tract of land that could be sold and the proceeds applied to the village. I thought it would be worth about $200,000, but it was later appraised at $820,000. She also gave $100,000 in cash to the glory of our Lord. Then a couple who had heard about the ministry village in a church service came by to ask questions after the service. After I had explained everything, he turned to his wife and asked if she would like to think about it. She replied, "No, I've made up my mind." He turned to me and said, "We'll give $75,000." Some of these persons were not even church members, but the Holy Spirit prompted them to give generously.

As persons made these commitments, I announced to the church what the Holy Spirit was doing without mentioning any names. One by one, contributors came forward. Because God's Spirit was already at work raising the money, I didn't want to interfere. I announced that we would not have a fund-raiser. Instead, at the end of the month we would have a special Sunday when persons could make pledges. I preached about our ministries for four consecutive Sundays and then invited members to make commitments according to the Spirit's leadership. The people committed $2,000,000, including the land. This was the result of God's movement among His people. Never ask, Can we afford it? Ask instead, Is it God's will? If it's God's will, He can afford it!

A wonderful couple from another church offered us $25,000 to start a Children's Shelter. In less than three months we began this ministry. After a story about the shelter appeared in the newspaper, a bank officer called to offer $35,000 from a trust fund. So $60,000 was given to us to start a ministry without asking for it. God provides the resources. Where He guides, He provides.

A woman in our congregation felt that we should do more than preach against abortion by providing an alternative. She and another woman gave $5,000, with which we began our Pregnancy-Care Ministry. God always provides.

Don: If a pastor or another leader asked you how to start ministry evangelism, what advice would you give?

Charles: A pastor or leader needs to take several important steps to lead a church to win persons to Christ by ministering to their needs. First, he must become convicted and convinced by the Holy Spirit that this is the direction the church needs to take. Pastors are incredibly busy and the expectations great. Because most of them have more to do than is possible, ministry evangelism cannot be just another program to add to the others that have to be done. Ministry evangelism is a way of looking at everything the church does. The leader must be convinced that God wants the church to take this direction. The leader must sense God's call to lead the church in ministry evangelism.

Second, the pastor or leader must bathe this matter in prayer. The church's work is not limited to what goes on inside the building on Sunday. Ministry evangelism is not business as usual. It requires church members to reexamine their priorities and to change the ways they do some things. Satan does not want the church to minister and win persons to Christ. Earnest, fervent prayer for God's vision, leadership, and power is essential.

Third, I suggest that the pastor or leader share his burden and vision with others in the church, for example, deacons and other church leaders. Many church members may already be open to the concept of ministry evangelism. Christians who have studied *Experiencing God, Disciple's Prayer Life,* or *MasterLife* may be interested in applying their training in practical ways. It is important to share this burden with others because ministry evangelism cannot be just the pastor's program. It will affect every member and every area of the church. A church cannot minister this way unless the members are committed to the idea. The pastor or leader should ask other members, especially other leaders, to join him in prayer about this crucial ministry. Eventually, the entire body will need to become involved; but leaders and other interested persons are the beginning points.

Next, I strongly recommend that a group be encouraged to study the course *Meeting Needs, Sharing Christ,* which complements this book. This six-week, small-group study will communicate to members the biblical mandate for ministry evangelism, enabling them to capture a vision of what their church can do through caring ministry. Participants will discover their spiritual gifts and will identify areas of ministry that are needed and possible for the church to implement. Each group member will complete an interactive workbook and will attend weekly group meetings to process what they have learned. The course also includes a leader guide, a videotape showing examples of ministries, and audiotapes, all of which are listed in appendix 3 of this book. A leader kit provides all of these resources in one package. The church should offer the course frequently to develop church members' awareness of ministry evangelism and to help them get started in ministry.

The next step is to determine what the church considers the greatest need in the community. It is usually advisable to start a ministry with low financial involvement but high personal involvement, such as a Homebound Ministry or a Latchkey Ministry. Do not start or plan a number of ministries in the beginning, but consider each need as it arises. I also suggest that you have one ministry that operates successfully before you begin another. You may have to keep some dreams on hold because of the high commitment required for finances and personnel, but the Lord will bring them to reality in His time.

Finally, I recommend that pastors and other church leaders begin to teach and model ministry evangelism through their roles. The pastor can use many insights in this book to prepare sermons that will call God's people to ministry. Leaders can teach these truths in Sunday School classes, Bible-study groups, and discipleship groups. Because people learn more from examples than from words, I encourage leaders, especially pastors, to begin ministering to hurting persons and winning persons to Christ as never before. Their examples will help convince the church that ministry evangelism is a priority.

Don: Charles, I know that winning persons to faith in Christ is the passion of your life. You and the great church you lead practice ministry evangelism that is biblical, practical, and at the heart of what God wants His church to do. What statement could you make that reflects your deepest convictions about winning persons to Christ through caring ministry?

Charles: In heaven we will be able to praise God more meaningfully, communicate with Him more powerfully, and live according to His perfect will. Only one thing can we do better on earth than in heaven, and that is telling a lost person about Jesus. Only here do we have that privilege, for the lost will not be in heaven. We must do everything possible to reach persons. This means involving ourselves in their hurt and brokenness. The brevity of time dictates this priority.

THE PROMISE OF HIS PRESENCE

The task of equipping God's people to be the body of Christ in a sinful, broken world is too great for human strength. We are not left to our own resources in this task. We are promised God's presence and power as we seek to lead His church to minister.

A. J. Gordon, a distinguished pastor in the late 19th century, related a powerful experience in his sermon "How Christ Came to Church." While putting the final touches on his sermon one Saturday evening, Gordon fell asleep and dreamed that he was in his pulpit before the congregation. Just as he was ready to begin his sermon, he noticed a stranger enter the sanctuary and walk down the left aisle, apparently looking for a seat. Finally, about halfway to the front, a man offered a seat to the stranger. As Gordon began to preach, he found that his eyes were riveted on the visitor. Although he tried to divert his attention from the stranger, he found that he could not stop looking at him.

In the dream Gordon wondered who this stranger could be and resolved to find out. As soon as the service was over, the preacher rushed to find the man, only to discover that he was gone. The man who had offered the stranger a seat was still in the aisle of the church, so Gordon asked him: "Can you tell me who the stranger was who sat in your pew this morning?" Surprised, the man replied: "Why, do you not know that man? It was Jesus of Nazareth."

Gordon expressed deep disappointment that he had not been able to speak to the distinguished guest. The church member responded: "Oh, do not be troubled. He has been here today, and no doubt He will come again."

When the preacher awakened from his dream, he could not forget those words: "He has been here today, and no doubt He will come again." The experience, although a dream, became a turning point in the great preacher's life. Reflecting on his dream and the scriptural promise that Jesus is always in the midst of His people, he wrote: "Thus it is made plain that the Lord Himself is truly though invisibly here in the midst of every company of disciples gathered anyplace in His name."[8] We may never experience such a powerful dream or vision, but the truth is that Jesus is always with His people. He is with us as we worship, as we discover our gifts, as we grow in discipleship, as we witness to His saving power, and as we touch persons' lives in His name. Our calling is to recognize His presence and to share His love with a hurting, sinful, broken humanity.

---

[1] Available for $5 each from the Discipleship Training Department; Baptist State Convention of North Carolina; P. O. Box 1107; Cary, NC 27512-1107.
[2] Chip Alford, "Teaching the Bible, Meeting Needs," *Facts & Trends*, December 1993, 5.
[3] For more information write to Church Study Course; the Sunday School Board of the Southern Baptist Convention; 127 Ninth Avenue, North; Nashville, TN 37234.
[4] Bill Hull, *Can We Save the Evangelical Church?* (Grand Rapids: Revell, 1993), 86.
[5] Ibid.
[6] Ibid., 87.
[7] George Barna, *The Power of Vision* (Ventura: Regal Books, 1992), 16.
[8] A. J. Gordon, *A. J. Gordon*, vol. 8 in *Great Pulpit Masters* (New York: Fleming H. Revell Company, 1951), 245–49.

1

Inventory of Spiritual Gifts

A NOTE TO CHURCH LEADERS

This inventory[1] is provided for your awareness and personal completion. It is copyrighted and therefore must not be duplicated for your church members. However, the instrument is also included in *Meeting Needs, Sharing Christ Member Book* (item 7200-43), available from the Customer Service Center; 127 Ninth Avenue, North; Nashville, TN 37234; 1-800-458-2772. Members who are studying the course in a group will complete the inventory in their member books as a part of that study.

DIRECTIONS

The inventory of spiritual gifts consists of 86 items. Some items reflect concrete actions, other items are descriptive traits, and still others are statements of beliefs.

As you read each item in the inventory, choose one of the following responses.

5	Highly characteristic of me or definitely true for me
4	Most of the time would describe me or be true for me
3	Frequently characteristic of me or true for me—about 50 percent of the time
2	Occasionally characteristic of me or true for me—about 25 percent of the time
1	Not at all characteristic of me or definitely untrue for me

In the blank beside each item place the number corresponding to the response that most accurately describes you.

Do not spend too much time on any one item. This is not a test, so there are no wrong answers. Usually, your immediate response is best.

Give an answer for each item. Do not skip any items.

The Inventory

_____ 1. I have the ability to organize ideas, resources, time, and persons effectively.

_____ 2. I am willing to study and prepare for the task of teaching.

_____ 3. I am able to relate God's truths to specific situations.

_____ 4. I inspire persons to right actions by pointing out the blessings of this path.

_____ 5. I have a God-given ability to help others grow in their faith.

_____ 6. I possess a special ability to communicate the truth of salvation.

_____ 7. I am sensitive to persons' hurts.

_____ 8. I experience joy in meeting needs through sharing possessions.

_____ 9. I enjoy study.

_____ 10. I have delivered God's messages of warning and judgment.

_____ 11. I am able to sense the true motivation of persons and movements.

_____ 12. I trust God in difficult situations.

_____ 13. I have a strong desire to contribute to the establishment of new churches.

_____ 14. I feel that God has used me as the agent in a supernatural event.

_____ 15. I enjoy doing things for persons in need.

_____ 16. I am sensitive to persons who suffer physical, mental, or emotional sickness.

_____ 17. I can delegate and assign meaningful work.

_____ 18. I have an ability and a desire to teach.

_____ 19. I am usually able to analyze a situation correctly.

___ 20. I have a tendency to encourage and reward others.

___ 21. I am willing to take the initiative in helping other Christians grow in their faith.

___ 22. I am unafraid to share with lost persons.

___ 23. I am acutely aware of such emotions as loneliness, pain, fear, and anger in others.

___ 24. I am a cheerful giver.

___ 25. I spend time researching facts.

___ 26. I feel that I have a message from God to deliver to others.

___ 27. I can recognize when a person is genuine/honest.

___ 28. I am willing to yield to God's will rather than to question and waver.

___ 29. I would like to be more active in taking the gospel to persons in other lands.

___ 30. Doing things for persons in need makes me happy.

___ 31. I am willing to be an instrument in healing others' physical, emotional, and mental hurts.

___ 32. I am successful in getting a group to do its work joyfully.

___ 33. I have the ability to plan learning approaches.

___ 34. I have been able to offer solutions to spiritual problems others face.

___ 35. I can identify persons who need encouragement.

___ 36. I have trained Christians to be more obedient disciples of Christ.

___ 37. I am willing to do whatever is necessary for others to come to Christ.

___ 38. I am drawn to persons who are hurting.

___ 39. I am a generous giver.

___ 40. I am able to discover new truths.

___ 41. I have spiritual insights from Scripture about issues and persons that compel me to speak out.

___ 42. I can sense when a person is acting in accordance with God's will.

___ 43. I can trust in God even when conditions look dark.

___ 44. I have a strong desire to take the gospel to places where it has never been heard.

___ 45. Others have testified of God's working in miraculous ways in the lives of persons to whom I have ministered.

___ 46. I enjoy helping persons.

___ 47. I understand scriptural teachings about healing.

___ 48. I have been able to make effective and efficient plans for accomplishing a group's goals.

___ 49. I understand the variety of ways persons learn.

___ 50. Fellow Christians often consult me when they are struggling to make difficult decisions.

___ 51. I think about ways I can comfort and encourage others in my congregation.

___ 52. I am able to give spiritual direction to others.

___ 53. I am able to present the gospel to lost persons in such a way that they accept the Lord and His salvation.

___ 54. I possess an unusual capacity to understand the feelings of persons in distress.

___ 55. I have a strong sense of stewardship based on the recognition of God's ownership of all things.

___ 56. I know where to get information.

_____ 57. I have delivered to other persons messages that have come directly from God.

_____ 58. I can sense when a person is acting under God's leadership.

_____ 59. I try to be in God's will continually.

_____ 60. I feel that I should take the gospel to persons who have beliefs different from mine.

_____ 61. I have faith that God can do the impossible in a needy situation.

_____ 62. I love to do things for others.

_____ 63. I am skilled in setting forth positive and precise steps of action.

_____ 64. I explain Scripture in such a way that others understand it.

_____ 65. I can usually see spiritual solutions to problems.

_____ 66. I am glad when persons who need comfort, consolation, encouragement, and counsel seek my help.

_____ 67. I am able to nurture others.

_____ 68. I feel at ease in sharing Christ with nonbelievers.

_____ 69. I recognize the signs of stress and distress in others.

_____ 70. I desire to give generously and unpretentiously to worthwhile projects and ministries.

_____ 71. I can organize facts into meaningful relationships.

_____ 72. God gives me messages to deliver to His people.

_____ 73. I am able to sense whether persons are being honest when they describe their religious experiences.

_____ 74. I try to be available for God to use.

_____ 75. I enjoy presenting the gospel to persons of other cultures or backgrounds.

___ 76. God has used me in miraculous answers to prayer.

___ 77. I enjoy doing little things that help others.

___ 78. I can plan a strategy and "bring others aboard."

___ 79. I can give a clear, uncomplicated presentation.

___ 80. I have been able to apply biblical truths to the specific needs of my church.

___ 81. God has used me to encourage others to live Christlike lives.

___ 82. I have sensed the need to help others become more effective in their ministries.

___ 83. I like to talk about Jesus with persons who do not know Him.

___ 84. I have a wide range of study resources.

___ 85. I feel assured that a situation will change for God's glory even when the situation seems impossible.

___ 86. I am aware that God still heals persons as He did in biblical times.

SCORING YOUR INVENTORY

1. For each gift listed on the following pages, place in the box the number of the response that you gave to each item indicated.
2. For each gift add the numbers in the boxes and put the total in the box labeled "Total."
3. For each gift divide the total by the number indicated and place the result in the box labeled "Score." (Round each number to one decimal place, such as 3.7.) This is your score for the gift.

LEADERSHIP	TEACHING	KNOWLEDGE	WISDOM
☐	☐	☐	☐
Item 1	Item 2	Item 9	Item 3
+	+	+	+
☐	☐	☐	☐
Item 17	Item 18	Item 25	Item 19
+	+	+	+
☐	☐	☐	☐
Item 32	Item 33	Item 40	Item 34
+	+	+	+
☐	☐	☐	☐
Item 48	Item 49	Item 56	Item 50
+	+	+	+
☐	☐	☐	☐
Item 63	Item 64	Item 71	Item 65
+	+	+	+
☐	☐	☐	☐
Item 78	Item 79	Item 84	Item 80
=	=	=	=
☐	☐	☐	☐
Total	Total	Total	Total
÷ 6	÷ 6	÷ 6	÷ 6
=	=	=	=
☐	☐	☐	☐
Score	Score	Score	Score

PROPHECY	**SPIRITUAL DISCERNMENT**	**EXHORTATION**	**SHEPHERDING**
☐	☐	☐	☐
Item 10	Item 11	Item 4	Item 5
+	+	+	+
☐	☐	☐	☐
Item 26	Item 27	Item 20	Item 21
+	+	+	+
☐	☐	☐	☐
Item 41	Item 42	Item 35	Item 36
+	+	+	+
☐	☐	☐	☐
Item 57	Item 58	Item 51	Item 52
+	+	+	+
☐	☐	☐	☐
Item 72	Item 73	Item 66	Item 67
=	=	+	+
☐	☐	☐	☐
Total	Total	Item 81	Item 82
÷ 5	÷ 5	=	=
=	=	☐	☐
☐	☐	Total	Total
Score	Score	÷ 6	÷ 6
		=	=
		☐	☐
		Score	Score

FAITH	EVANGELISM	APOSTLESHIP	MIRACLES
☐	☐	☐	☐
Item 12	Item 6	Item 13	Item 14
+	+	+	+
☐	☐	☐	☐
Item 28	Item 22	Item 29	Item 45
+	+	+	+
☐	☐	☐	☐
Item 43	Item 37	Item 44	Item 61
+	+	+	+
☐	☐	☐	☐
Item 59	Item 53	Item 60	Item 76
+	+	+	=
☐	☐	☐	☐
Item 74	Item 68	Item 75	Total
+	+	=	÷ 4
☐	☐	☐	=
Item 85	Item 83	Total	☐
=	=	÷ 5	Score
☐	☐	=	
Total	Total	☐	
÷ 6	÷ 6	Score	
=	=		
☐	☐		
Score	Score		

HELPS	MERCY	GIVING	HEALING
☐	☐	☐	☐
Item 15	Item 7	Item 8	Item 16
+	+	+	+
☐	☐	☐	☐
Item 30	Item 23	Item 24	Item 31
+	+	+	+
☐	☐	☐	☐
Item 46	Item 38	Item 39	Item 47
+	+	+	+
☐	☐	☐	☐
Item 62	Item 54	Item 55	Item 86
+	+	+	=
☐	☐	☐	☐
Item 77	Item 69	Item 70	Total
=	=	=	÷ 4
☐	☐	☐	=
Total	Total	Total	☐
÷ 5	÷ 5	÷ 5	Score
=	=	=	
☐	☐	☐	
Score	Score	Score	

Ideas for Ministry

The following ideas suggest possible areas of ministry in which churches and individuals can become involved. The possibilities for ministry are endless. This list is meant only to help you get started. Some ideas are more applicable than others to your church and community.

Some ministries require the enlistment of professionals, such as doctors, nurses, or dentists. Church leaders should check state and local codes and regulations before beginning certain ministries. Other ministries involve more liability than others. Church leaders should make certain their insurance provides coverage for all ministries.

Some ministry ideas suggest or allow the use of particular resources. These resources are listed in appendix 3, "Resources for Ministry."

Adequate promotion is a major contributor to the success of most ministries. Local newspapers, church newsletters, community bulletin boards, billboards, letters to civic groups, and fliers posted in places of business (with permission) are possible means of promotion.

MINISTRIES TO PARENTS AND MARRIED COUPLES

Parents' day out. Provide child care one or more days a week. Funded by a small charge to parents and by scholarships.

New parents. Provide baby-sitting for new parents.

Family seminars. Provide help with family issues such as discipline, safety, and nutrition.

Couples' supper club. Organize groups of couples to meet in homes regularly to eat together and enjoy Christian fellowship.

Marriage-enrichment seminars, studies, and retreats. Provide help for married couples in developing strong marriages and advertise in the community. See appendix 3 for resources.

Parenting seminars, studies, and retreats. Provide help for enriching parenting skills and advertise in the community. See appendix 3 for resources.

Cradle Roll. Visit in the home of new parents, enroll the baby, and give a pink or blue Bible.

Premarital counseling and seminars. Provide help for couples considering or preparing for marriage. See appendix 3 for resources.

MINISTRIES TO WOMEN
Pregnancy care. Provide free pregnancy tests, counseling, and prenatal care. Include nutritional and parenting help.

Shepherding for expectant mothers. Provide temporary care in the homes of church families for pregnant women who have no place to live.

New mothers. Prepare and deliver packets containing such items as a bib, a pink or blue Bible, a coupon for a home-cooked meal that will be delivered to the home when needed, *ParentLife* magazine, and information about the church.

Women's care. Provide housing, protection, and care for displaced, endangered, or abused women.

Single mothers. Provide practical help such as encouragement, fellowship, seminars, and emergency child care.

Clothing. Provide appropriate work clothing for indigent women seeking employment.

MINISTRIES TO MEN
Rescue mission. Provide help for men in crisis because of homelessness, alcoholism, drug addiction, or other problems.

Single fathers. Provide practical help such as encouragement, fellowship, seminars, and emergency child care.

Clothing. Provide appropriate work clothing for indigent men seeking employment.

MINISTRIES TO CHILDREN
Day care. Provide a regular program of care funded by tuition costs.

School clothing. Collect, purchase, and distribute school clothing for underprivileged children.

Hospital activity packs. Prepare and deliver packs to hospitalized children with such items as Bibles, coloring books, crayons, small stuffed animals, puzzle books, and Christian books. Be sure to check with hospital personnel.

Children's care. Provide temporary shelter, food, and protection for children in crisis.

Latchkey ministry. Provide before- and after-school care for a small fee.

Foster care. Provide certified homes to care for displaced children.

Summer day camp. Provide an opportunity for disadvantaged children to learn and grow. Include recreation, Bible study, and evangelism.

Vacation Bible School. Make Bible study and activities available to children, using a planned curriculum. See appendix 3 for resources.

Backyard Bible Clubs. Organize neighborhood Bible clubs for children. See appendix 3 for resources.

MINISTRIES TO YOUTH AND STUDENTS
Tutoring. Provide a free after-school program to help students with academic problems.

Youth prayer breakfast. Prepare a free breakfast for youth once a week, providing Christian fellowship and witness.

Students away. Provide literature, personal letters, and encouragement through volunteers.

Campus reading room. Make a reading room available near a school, using volunteers to interact with students and to answer questions.

Seekers. Invite students to a forum at which they ask questions about Christianity and interact with Christian students.

Christian school. Provide quality education in a Christian context.

Teen drivers. Offer a car-care-and-safety course, including a Christian testimony.

Teen club. Provide Friday- and Saturday-night social events that include food, fun, and a Christian witness. This activity must be carefully planned and supervised.

MINISTRIES TO SENIOR ADULTS
Adult day care. Provide for those who need care while adult children fulfill other responsibilities.

Home meal delivery. Provide hot meals.

The homebound. Provide visitation, spiritual help, and practical ministry to those unable to attend church services.

Nursing homes. Plan worship, Bible study, prayer, visitation, and encouragement for residents of nursing homes.

Grandparenting seminars. Offer seminars on grandparenting and advertise in the community. See appendix 3 for resources.

Transportation. Provide transportation for grocery shopping, medical appointments, and church attendance.

Activities. Plan regular programs of meaningful study and activity.

Retirement centers. Provide worship services for retirement centers including music and testimonies.

Shopping-and-errand service. Run errands and shop for the homebound.

Lawn care. Provide lawn care permanently or temporarily as needed.

MINISTRIES TO SINGLE ADULTS
Home care. Provide home repair, especially for widows, elderly persons, and single mothers.

Car repair. Offer automobile repair, especially for widows, elderly persons, and single mothers.

MINISTRIES TO SPECIAL NEEDS
Deaf persons. Provide a Sunday School class and a Discipleship Training group and interpretation of worship services.

Blind persons. Provide tapes of worship services and other events.

Caregivers. Provide temporary relief for caregivers of persons with special needs.

HEALTH-CARE MINISTRIES
Mammogram screening. Provide a mobile unit to offer mammograms to women who cannot afford them otherwise.

Dental-care unit. Provide dental care to indigent persons through a mobile unit.

Vision clinic. Provide eye care for needy persons through a mobile unit.

Christian health program. Offer weekly sessions at the church. See appendix 3 for resources.

Aerobics. Offer aerobics classes at the church. The trained leader should be sensitive to participants' needs and should provide time for prayer requests.

Persons with AIDS. Provide help and encouragement for patients and their families.

Health screening. Conduct screenings for blood pressure and cholesterol in disadvantaged neighborhoods.

Bloodmobile. Have the Red Cross bloodmobile come to the church. Advertise hours to the community. Provide refreshments and Christian tracts for blood donors.

Flu shots. Provide free flu shots at the church for the community, working with the local health department.

SPORTS MINISTRIES
Athletic events. Sponsor an event such as a walk/run or a softball tournament for the purpose of witnessing.

Young athletes. Provide clinics for young baseball, soccer, football, and tennis players. Have a Christian athlete give a testimony.

Golfers. Sponsor a golf tournament, inviting persons who need Christ to participate. Share a Christian testimony.

Athletes. Hold a pizza party for local high-school or college teams with opportunities for sharing Christ.

Athletic teams. Offer exercise, competition, fellowship, and a Christian witness through team sports.

After-game celebrations. Provide food and fun for high-school teams in a Christian atmosphere.

MINISTRIES TO THE COMMUNITY
Food baskets. Prepare and distribute baskets of food to needy families during holidays and at other times.

Christmas toy store. Purchase and collect new toys and other children's items and arrange the merchandise like a store. Invite parents who cannot afford to buy Christmas gifts for their children to come and select items free. Provide a Christian witness to the parents before they leave.

Financial seminars. Offer help with debt, budgeting, and planning.

Home Bible study. Invite neighbors to a home Bible study on a weeknight or a weekday morning.

Income-tax assistance. Provide free help with income-tax preparation at the church during specific, advertised hours.

Bereavement. Provide meals and other services for families or individuals in bereavement.

Sympathy notes. Mail a sympathy note to the family of every person whose name appears in the obituary column of the newspaper. This activity could be done by a group such as a Sunday School class or by an individual.

Financial assistance. Distribute funds to persons with basic financial needs such as rent, utilities, food, and prescriptions.

Food pantry. Distribute food from donations and government commodities.

Furniture barn. Distribute donated furniture and other household items.

Clothes closet. Distribute clean, wearable, used clothing.

Families of prisoners. Provide encouragement, spiritual help, and physical resources for families who have loved ones in prison.

Personal-care kits for prisoners. Include toothpaste, toothbrush, soap, shaving cream, candy, gum, and Christian literature. Be sure to check with institutional authorities before assembling the kits.

Prayer breakfasts. Invite community residents to pray for community needs once a week at the church or a local residence. Bible study could be included.

Shelter for the homeless. Provide church facilities in which homeless persons can sleep on cold or stormy nights.

Buses. Use church-owned or privately owned vehicles to provide transportation to church activities.

Prayer. Mobilize the church to pray for needs in the church and community. See appendix 3 for resources.

Truck stops. Provide Christian literature and fellowship for long-distance truck drivers.

Counseling. Provide group or individual counseling by professional counselors or by trained lay counselors. See appendix 3 for resources.

Decision counseling. Counsel persons making decisions for Christ. See appendix 3 for resources.

Holiday meals. Provide meals for the homeless on holidays or at other times.

Resorts. Offer Bible study or worship services at a nearby resort.

Prisoners. Provide visits, Bible study, worship, and literature to persons in prison.

Special events. Witness and minister at special community events. For example, provide a booth at a community festival and serve free beverages. Be sure to obtain permission first.

Literacy. Teach persons to read, in the process sharing Christ with them.

Christmas-gift wrapping. Provide free or inexpensive gift wrapping in a mall. Distribute tracts and witness.

Christian fellowship. Provide a block party with food, entertainment, and a Christian witness for persons in the neighborhood.

Crafts and cooking classes. Offer classes for the community. The leader should be sensitive to participants' needs and provide a time for prayer requests.

New residents. Provide kits for new residents including a city map; lists of hospitals, dentists, and physicians; shopping and school information; a gift certificate for a meal at a local restaurant or a coupon for a home-cooked meal; information about the church; and a Christian magazine (see appendix 3 for resources). Invite new residents to be guests at the church's Wednesday-night dinner.

Fellowship lunch. Invite working persons to a fellowship lunch once a week that includes Bible study and prayer.

Public-service personnel. Host an appreciation day for law-enforcement personnel and firefighters.

Bibles. Give Bibles to groups such as college students, military personnel, firefighters, members of athletic teams, law-enforcement officers, or nurses.

24-hour prayer line. Provide and advertise a telephone line that is staffed 24 hours a day. Receive prayer requests and pray. See appendix 3 for prayer resources.

Hospitality. Provide meals in family settings for students, military personnel, and businesspersons away from home.

Sewing and knitting. Make lap robes, booties, and other articles to give away.

Snow removal. Recruit volunteers for a snow-removal brigade that services walks and driveways at the homes of the elderly, single mothers, the disabled, and non-Christians. Leave a note stating that this act was done in Jesus' love.

Christian tapes. Develop a library that includes audiotapes on biblical subjects, life issues, and music. Make the tapes available to church members to share with unchurched family members and friends.

Disaster relief. Develop teams and resources to work with denominational and community agencies to assist victims of disasters.

Car wash. Provide a free car wash, accepting no payment other than thanks. Serve lemonade to customers. Share that Christ's love is the reason for offering this service.

Church computer bulletin board. Reach out to the growing population of computer users who subscribe to on-line networks.

Birthday cards. Send birthday greetings with Christian messages to as many unchurched persons as possible.

MINISTRIES TO INTERNATIONALS
Language skills. Teach persons to read and speak English. Bible study and worship in the native language could also be provided.

Women's cultural fellowship. Plan a weekly or monthly fellowship time for women from different countries to learn about American culture and one another's culture. Provide assistance with tasks such as grocery shopping.

Home hospitality. Provide meals in homes for families or individuals who have recently arrived from other countries.

MINISTRIES THROUGH CHURCH PROGRAMS
Musical productions. Use seasonal musical productions such as a living Christmas tree to provide a Christian witness.

Saturday Sunday School. Provide a Saturday Bible-study program for children from disadvantaged circumstances. See appendix 3 for resources.

Sidewalk Sunday School. Use a portable classroom to take Bible study to neighborhoods in the inner city or in unchurched areas. See appendix 3 for resources.

Music. Use choirs, ensembles, and other groups to involve children, youth, adults, and senior adults in ministry. Have groups perform in public places, providing the opportunity to share a Christian witness.

Drama. Use drama to involve interested persons and to present the gospel.

Puppet. Use puppetry to involve those who wish to present the gospel in this manner, especially to children.

SUPPORT-GROUP MINISTRIES
Divorce recovery. Provide help for persons who are divorced or who face divorce. See appendix 3 for resources.

Sexual abuse. Provide help for persons who are victims of sexual abuse. See appendix 3 for resources.

Grief recovery. Provide help for persons who have experienced losses in their lives. See appendix 3 for resources.

Chemical addiction. Provide help for persons who are recovering from addiction to alcohol or other drugs. See appendix 3 for resources.

Codependency. Provide help for persons who are dealing with issues of co-dependency. See appendix 3 for resources.

Eating disorders. Provide help for persons recovering from eating disorders. See appendix 3 for resources.

MINISTRIES TO PERSONS IN CRISIS
Rape crisis. Provide immediate support and practical help for rape victims.

24-hour crisis line. Provide a telephone number persons in crisis can call at any time to receive counseling. The number should be published in the community, for example, on a billboard.

Crisis counseling. Provide immediate crisis-intervention counseling for persons in crisis.

Resources for Ministry

Unless otherwise noted, products are available from the Customer Service Center; 127 Ninth Avenue, North; Nashville, TN 37234; 1-800-458-2772; from Baptist Book Stores; and from Lifeway Christian Stores.

MINISTRY EVANGELISM
Meeting Needs, Sharing Christ: Ministry Evangelism in Today's New Testament Church by Donald A. Atkinson and Charles L. Roesel
- Member book, item 7200-43
- Leader guide, item 7200-42
- Videocassettes, item 7700-40
- Audiocassettes, item 7700-41
- Leader kit, item 7700-42

Conspiracy of Kindness by Steve Sjogren; Servant Publications; P.O. Box 8617; Ann Arbor, MI 48107

DISCOVERY GROUPS
Breaking the Cycle of Hurtful Family Experiences by Robert McGee, Pat Springle, Jim Craddock, and Susan Lanford
- Member book, item 7210-74
- Leader guide, item 7212-74

Search for Significance, LIFE® Support Group Series Edition by Robert S. McGee
- Member book, item 7264-62
- Leader guide, item 7269-62

Untangling Relationships: A Christian Perspective on Codependency by Pat Springle and Susan Lanford
- Member book, item 7202-73
- Leader guide, item 7203-73

SUPPORT GROUPS

A Time for Healing: Coming to Terms with Your Divorce by Harold Ivan Smith
- Member book, item 7200-28
- Facilitator guide, item 7200-29

Conquering Chemical Dependency: A Christ-Centered 12-Step Process by Robert S. McGee and Dale McCleskey with Pat Springle and Susan Joiner
- Member book, item 7206-33
- Facilitator guide, item 7207-33

Conquering Chemical Dependency: First Steps to A Christ-Centered 12-Step Process by Robert S. McGee and Dale McCleskey with Pat Springle and Susan Joiner, item 7213-94

Conquering Codependency: A Christ-Centered 12-Step Process by Pat Springle and Dale McCleskey
- Member book, item 7200-33
- Facilitator guide, item 7201-33

Conquering Eating Disorders: A Christ-Centered 12-Step Process by Robert McGee, William Drew Mountcastle, and Jim and Annette Florence
- Member book, item 7204-73
- Facilitator guide, item 7205-73

Family and Friends: Helping the Person You Care About in Recovery by Larry Pillow with David Walley
- Member book, item 7200-26
- Facilitator guide by Dale McCleskey, item 7200-24

First Place: A Christ-Centered Health Program
- Member notebook, item 7227-72
- Leader guide, item 7228-72
- *Orientation/Food Exchange Video,* item 7241-72
- *First Place Favorites* recipe book, item 7271-72
- *Nutrition for God's Temple,* item 7200-14
- *Study Guide Supplement Pack,* item 7200-12
- Bible-study packs:
  - *Everyday Victory for Everyday People,* item 7256-72
  - *Giving Christ First Place,* item 7243-72
  - *Life That Wins,* item 7257-72
  - *Life Under Control,* item 7260-72

LIFE₍ₑ₎ Support Group Series Training Video, item 7700-24

LIFE® *Support Group Series Leader Handbook,* compiled by Johnny Jones, item 7268-02

Making Peace with Your Past by Tim Sledge
  • Member book, item 7636-14
  • Facilitator guide, item 7616-14

Moving Beyond Your Past by Tim Sledge
  • Member book, item 7023-03
  • Facilitator guide, item 7024-03

Quitting for Good: A Christ-Centered Approach to Nicotine Dependency by Fran McClain
  • Member book, item 7200-53
  • Facilitator guide, item 7200-54

Recovering from the Losses of Life: LIFE® *Support Group Series Edition* by H. Norman Wright and Kay W. Moore
  • Member book, item 7200-27
  • Facilitator guide, item 7200-25

Shelter from the Storm: Hope for Victims of Sexual Abuse by Cynthia Kubetin, James Mallory, and Jacque Truitt
  • Member book, item 7208-44
  • Facilitator guide, item 7209-44

WiseCounsel: Skills for Lay Counseling by John W. Drakeford and Claude V. King
  • Member book, item 7259-08
  • Leader guide, item 7791-08
  • Videocassette, item 8435-68

DISCIPLESHIP TRAINING
Experiencing God: Knowing and Doing the Will of God by Henry T. Blackaby and Claude V. King
  • Member book, item 7203-00
  • Leader guide, item 7225-00
  • *The Seven Realities of Experiencing God Video Series,* item 7700-44
  • *Experiencing God Audiocassettes,* item 5160-43
Age-group and language editions of *Experiencing God* are also available.

Additional Discipleship Training resources are produced by the Sunday School Board of the Southern Baptist Convention. For information about adult resources write to the Adult Discipleship and Family Department; the Sunday School Board; 127 Ninth Avenue, North; Nashville, TN 37234. To order materials, contact the Customer Service Center (see p. 169 for address).

MONEY MANAGEMENT
Master Your Money by Ron Blue
- Workbook, item 7288-43
- Video training kit, item 7287-43

PRAYER MINISTRY
Church Prayer Ministry Manual, compiled by T. W. Hunt, item 5130-33
- Video, item 8502-52

Disciple's Prayer Life: Walking in Fellowship with God by T. W. Hunt and Catherine Walker, item 7232-18

In God's Presence by T. W. Hunt and Claude V. King, item 7200-63

Watchman Prayer Ministry by Larry L. Thompson
- *Watchman Prayer Ministry Planning Kit,* item 7285-53
- *Watchman Prayer Guide,* item 7284-53
- *Watchman Prayer Ministry Display and Promotion Pack,* item 7286-53

NEW CHURCH MEMBERS
Basics for Baptists by Ernest E. Mosley, item 5130-21

DecisionTime: Commitment Counseling by Leonard Sanderson and Arthur H. Criscoe
- Notebook, item 7204-07
- Videocassette, item 8436-68

Survival Kit for Christians by Ralph W. Neighbour, Jr.
- Member book, item 5131-31
- Leader guide, item 5141-32

Welcome to God's Family, item 9218-01

WITNESS TRAINING
Witnessing Through Your Relationships by Jack R. Smith and Jennifer Kennedy Dean
- Member book, item 7643-73
- Leader guide, item 7646-73

Learning to Share My Faith by Chuck Kelley
  • Member book, item 7200-30
  • Leader kit, item 7700-29

MARRIAGE AND FAMILY

Building Relationships: A Discipleship Guide for Married Couples by Gary Chapman
  • Couple guide, item 7200-35
  • Leader guide, item 7200-36

Christian Self-esteem: Parenting by Grace by Diana Garland, Kathryn Chapman, and Jerry Pounds
  • Parent guide, item 7802-01
  • Leader guide, item 7801-01

Communication and Intimacy: Covenant Marriage by Gary Chapman and Betty Hassler
  • Couple guide, item 7803-02
  • Leader notebook, item 7804-02

Counsel for the Nearly and Newly Married, item 5131-09

Covenant Marriage: Partnership and Commitment by Diana Garland and Betty Hassler
  • Couple guide, item 7215-07
  • Leader notebook, item 7226-07

Christian Sex Education Series
  • *Boys and Girls—Alike and Different* by Ellen Chambers (ages 4–7), item 7805-43
  • *My Body and Me* by Norma Stevens (ages 8–9), item 7806-43
  • *Sexuality: God's Gift* by Ann Cannon (ages 14–17), item 7808-43
  • *Sex! What's That?* by Susan Lanford (ages 10–13), item 7807-43
  • *Parents and Church Leaders Guide* compiled by Jimmy Hester, item 7810-43
  • *Christian Sex Education Set*, item 7811-43
  • *True Love Waits Thru the Roof Planning Kit*, item 5620-50

The Decision Is Yours: Help for Senior Adults and Their Families with Housing Options by David Jakes, item 7800-03

The Five Love Languages by Gary Chapman
- Video pack, item 7700-45
- Viewing guide/love-language inventory, item 7200-37

Grandparenting by Grace by Irene M. Endicott and C. Ferris Jordan
- Member book, item 7200-01
- Leader guide, item 7200-02

Growing Older, Growing Wiser by Dolph Curb, Ben Dickerson, Carolyn Spears, and Robert Trotter, item 5131-14

Husbands and Wives: The Best of Friends by Otis and Deigie Andrews, item 7200-55

Marriage Mentors: Guiding and Encouraging Couples to a Healthy Marriage Relationship by Bob and Yvonne Turnbull, item 7200-40

Marriage Savers Resource Collection: Proven Ways to Prevent Divorce by Michael McManus, item 7901-01
- *Insuring Marriage: 25 Proven Ways to Prevent Divorce* (member book) by Michael McManus, item 7800-01

Parenting by Grace: Discipline and Spiritual Growth by Dixie Ruth Crase and Arthur H. Criscoe
- Parent guide, item 7764-06
- Leader guide, item 7765-06

CHRISTIAN MAGAZINES
Christian Single, item 1806
Experiencing God, item 1810
Home Life, item 1801
Journey, item 1809
Living with Teenagers, item 1803
Mature Living, item 1802
ParentLife, item 1808
All magazines listed are published monthly.

SUNDAY SCHOOL, VACATION BIBLE SCHOOL, AND BACKYARD BIBLE CLUB
A complete line of materials for all age groups is published by the Sunday School Board of the Southern Baptist Convention. For information write to the Bible Teaching-Reaching Division; the Sunday School Board; 127 Ninth Avenue, North; Nashville, TN 37234. To order materials, contact the

Customer Service Center (see p. 169 for address).

ORGANIZATIONS
First Baptist Church
220 North 13th Street
Leesburg, FL 34748
904-787-1005

The Home Mission Board of the Southern Baptist Convention
1350 Spring Street, NW
Atlanta, GA 30367-5601
Customer Service, 1-800-634-2462

New Covenant Baptist Church
Clyde McCants
P.O. Box 68
Rock Cave, WV 26234

Vineyard Community Church
Steve Sjogren
P.O. Box 46562
Cincinnati, OH 45246
Fax, 513-671-2041